# Practically Nothing

Transforming Your Practice
of Centering Prayer
through the Wisdom
of Mystical Nothingness

OCT 20

## Table of Contents

Unnamed Meditation

Introduction

A Brief Introduction to Centering Prayer

Chapter 1: Why Nothing?

Chapter 2: The Christian Tradition of Nothingness

Chapter 3: Nothingness in the Practice of Centering Prayer

Chapter 4: Self-Reflection: The Objectifying Thought

Chapter 5: Nothingness in Daily Life

Chapter 6: The Experience of Failure in the Contemplative Life

Chapter 7: The Hiddenness of Contemplation

Chapter 8: Prayer in Secret: Just Nothing

Appendix I: Instruction Prayer for Deepening into Mystical Nothingness

Appendix II: Commentary on "Instruction Prayer for Deepening into Mystical Nothingness"

*Author's Note: All Biblical quotes are taken from the New American Bible translation.*

## Unnamed Meditation

In Jesus Crucified God reveals Godself as nothing. On the cross God dies to being God, to *being* at all. At the same time, God and I are one, always and forever - grace given gratuitously. My center, my deepest self, is divine. Since God is nothing, I am nothing. The way to God is nothingness. God invites me into this divine play, the joy of letting myself be reduced to what I have always been: nothing. I am to be crucified with Christ and so know the divine bliss, but know beyond my mind by knowing nothing. And so, I allow you, O God, to annihilate all distinction and all being and open me to the realization that I am the self-same nothing.

Nothingness means death to God and self. On the cross God dies to God, and invites us to die as well. God invites us to die with God to enter the fullness of life. Dying to self. What does this phrase mean? It lies at the heart of Jesus' teaching. He seems to command it - die to yourself. And yet, to me, it is an oddly gentle invitation: let yourself go. Let yourself go into God; let your very self dissolve into the void of godless nothing. Die, dissolve, disappear. It is actually rather simple - dare I say easy! In silence, in solitude, I let go of all thought and all feeling and all desire. I just drop it, allowing all of it to fade away. It may still be there as background noise. That's ok. All I do is let myself sink into the nothingness beneath ego, mental habits, fear, anxiety, depression, attachments, and even happiness. The mystery lies beneath all that, beneath my very self. In this pure prayer, I cultivate the null state. I allow the divine nothingness to surface from within, from deeper than consciousness: the sheer gratuity of vacant nullity, the utter joy of mindless oblivion. Contemplative prayer is sinking into the indistinct nothingness. In contemplative practice allow non-thinking nothing, selfless nothing, crucified

5

nothing, godless nothing, simply and purely and only nothing. Contemplation is the realization of nothing in nothing as nothing beyond nothing, for God is nothing. Blessed nothingness beyond God! In contemplative silence: nothingness.

Mystery, pure mystery! And, the mystery is, in some unfathomable sense, me. This is all I want. This is all I desire: to dissolve into the incomprehensible mystery of God beyond God, to disappear into the good and gracious nothing. What sheer joy and utter ecstasy! Such freedom and aliveness! In becoming nothing I discover myself and everyone and everything else! Infinite oneness! And yet, *and yet*! I am not lost in some ephemeral haze, some esoteric mist. I am here, now - now, here, nowhere. I am grounded in the ground that has no ground. In discovering the nothingness as my deepest me, I realize I am love, all is love. Ultimately, and even amidst all my trauma and tragedy - all my people's suffering - all is ok. This dying has led to life: love and joy and beauty, here and now. So, nothingness is real, life-giving, overflowing with divine happiness. Crucifixion IS resurrection: nothingness IS love, gratuitous and free. But still the challenge, perhaps daunting, of sinking into the indistinct nothingness and so the harrowing implication of losing all that is me. It is a fierce letting go. Identify with no thing at all, nothing! Identify with vacant nullity. Hang upon the cross of annihilation unto the joyous revelation and realization of the nihil: I am nothing. The one who has become nothing in the eternal nothing has no knowledge of distinction. The indistinct nothingness is the identical sameness of self and God: one and the same nothing.

Nullified my deepest self is revealed as the vacant nihility of the non-God beyond awareness and divinity. I let self be the same as nothingness. And in and from nothingness awakens the non-I, the nihil-I. Desert nothing, empty and vast and clear. My self must be annihilated to realize nothingness beyond God. This is the sameness of the null state. Utter blessing, freedom untold and joy beyond joy! For, divine nothingness is my nothingness and my nothingness is divine nothingness.

Struck down to the ground, the one godless ground, I then rise, ready to accept and love all in the nihilistic ground of all reality, transcending being and consciousness. Jesus promised a hundredfold reward to those who leave everything. In dying to self and everything else, it all comes back as gift, sheer gift! Wondrous gift! The nothingness frees me to enjoy life as it is, to savor life - to taste reality fully: family, friends, a cup of coffee, the smell of the air, a blade of grass, a bird's gentle song, the sun, the blue sapphire sky. All gift! The gift of nothing. What clear oneness! And all it takes is the letting go of self into the nothingness beyond God.

But oh how names get in the way! We so easily suppose our names and our words contain the reality they point to: God, Jesus, Buddha, Allah, Brahman, Father, Mother, him, him, him - always we refer to God as "he, him!" I am tired of the *man*-made God, the father in the sky. I am appalled at the fighting and the violence surrounding the defense and upholding of one and only one name. Stop it. Stop being so dull, dim, one-dimensional, so utterly childish. I understand it and feel for those still in that frame of mind, but I must, I must, I must challenge it! The mystery transcends names and so we can use all names. It's all fair game! No theology or ideology can encompass the Godhead. No thought grasp the ungraspable. No mind can contain the wild divine oblivion beyond all names, theologies, experiences, and religions. But I won't let any name, any certitude, any idea, any theology, any ideology, any thought or feeling keep me from dying into the nothing, my infinite joy. I will sink. I will sink into the indistinct nothingness. For, annihilated in nothing I am nothing.

Annihilated in nothing,
I no longer exist.
Being is obliterated,
Self vanishes in the vacuum.
No perception, no awareness,
Everything becomes blank:
Anyone becomes no one.
Anybody becomes nobody.
God: nil, zilch, the not.
All return to the void,
Awakening to true identity:
Divine oblivion,
I am oblivion.
Divine nothing,
I am nothing.


Crucified with Christ I vanish into the void of godless nothing

# Introduction

Nothingness gives life, unfolding within us peace, freedom, and compassion. This is my testimony. When I sit down to pray, it is all nothing - nothing but nothing. My silent prayer lacks spiritual experiences and sweet religious feelings. Thoughts constantly buzz around in my head. Underneath, around, above, and within all the thoughts, however, resides nothingness. And the nothingness is pure joy. Through the nothingness I share in the desert experience of Jesus; I identify with the crucified-now-risen Christ. This is my witness: the nothing is good! The desert nothing is a lush paradise. All I want to do is share my joy.

This little book, therefore, is about this joy. In particular, it discusses the deepening of the practice and teaching of a Christian method of prayer called centering prayer, which is a contemplative practice that opens up to contemplation. According to Christian tradition, contemplation is a process of gradual (and sometimes not-so-gradual) awakening in prayer and daily life to our ever-present oneness with God. The Mystery of God reveals and gives this oneness in Jesus Christ and through the Holy Spirit. So, the ultimate purpose of this little book is to serve this spiritual awakening by offering some practical instruction from the Christian mystical tradition. In particular, I will focus on teachings from the Christian apophatic mystical tradition (this tradition is composed of Christian figures like Meister Eckhart, pseudo-Dionysius the Areopagite, the author of *The Cloud of Unknowing*, and St. John of the Cross) in conjunction with my own spiritual journey as expressed in the unnamed meditation above.

Christian apophatic mysticism reminds us God is mystery - beyond words, thoughts, experiences, and even being. And so, we must open to God beyond words, thoughts, emotions, and being. Down through the ages many have called this tradition the negative way to God. The negative way to God contrasts the positive way to God, which is a way of using images, feelings, experiences, words, names, and thinking to draw close to God. Christianity has called this positive way, "kataphatic mysticism." Christian apophatic mystics are not limited to the apophatic. They often vigorously make us of the kataphatic. They will pile on images of God, always aware that no image is absolutely definitive of the divine. Apophatic mysticism, though, leaves all images aside because it recognizes God is greater than all of it. Indeed, centering prayer emerges from apophatic mysticism. So, in line with this tradition, the teachings I present are summed up in one word: nothing. Prepare yourself for nothingness!

Through the years I have integrated this tradition into my own spirituality. So, I hope to connect and deepen the practice of centering prayer by unfolding my own reflections on nothingness while remaining grounded in the Christian tradition of apophatic mysticism. There are no obligations to start using the words, images, and concepts presented in this little book. Regardless of whether or not you, the reader, like negative images, metaphors, and concepts - which I will use throughout this little book - there is deep wisdom in the negative way. My prayer is that you absorb this wisdom for the deepening of your own practice and understanding of centering prayer, especially as it develops into pure contemplation.

( Now, it is imperative to avoid a damnable misunderstanding of the crucifying nothingness, of spiritual emptiness, of the cross in general. I do not mean for such a spirituality to be used to oppress any people by validating the passive acceptance of suffering. Do not interpret the nothingness to mean one must fatalistically put up with abuse, violence, or oppression of any kind - personal or social. In situations where there is violence, God desires peace; where there is oppression, God wants justice; where there is abuse, God needs it to stop. God unshackles us by reducing our slavery to nothing and giving birth to harmony and right relationship. In and through nothingness God liberates. God offers this to all in prayer.

I write this book mainly for people who practice centering prayer. I believe, however, that practitioners of other contemplative methods - such as John Main's Christian meditation, the Jesus Prayer, *lectio divina*, and Christian Zen - will benefit as well. But, perhaps you are brand new to the world of contemplative practice, and centering prayer in particular? If so, you can still profit from the insights of this little book. I recommend reading the next section of the preface, "A Brief Introduction to Centering Prayer," to discover the "what" and the "how" of centering prayer. Then, practice the prayer, at least a few times, before continuing with the rest of the book. This will give you an experiential basis for the teachings that follow. Knowing the practice from the inside will lead to a greater understanding of and appreciation for the teachings on nothingness.

In this little book, I build on what David Frenette has already taught concerning practice with the "sacred nothingness." In his book, *The Path of Centering Prayer*, Frenette discusses practicing centering prayer with the sacred nothingness as practicing without the help of a symbol - whether the word, the breath, or the glance. He says, "Pray with nothing - no thought, no symbol, no effort, no image."[1] He further describes practicing with the sacred nothingness as "Let everything be, just as it is, in God."[2] This is

---

[1] Frenette, David, *The Path of Centering Prayer*, Boulder, CO: Sounds True, 2012, 78.
[2] *Ibid.*, 94

masterful contemplative teaching. We will see how this little book builds on Frenette, expanding on his treatment while offering a different perspective.

I will talk about nothingness in eight chapters. To start, I will answer a simple question: why nothing?" Then chapter two will look more closely at the tradition of nothingness in Christianity, especially in Jesus and in apophatic mystics like Meister Eckhart and John of the Cross. Next, in chapter three, I will unpack the implications of nothingness for our practice of centering prayer. How we handle our thoughts and consent will be our core topics. Chapter four will be a consideration of the thought of self-reflection. Chapter five will outline and comment on the practice of nothingness in daily life - that is, beyond the time of meditation. Then, in chapter six, we will examine the issue of failure in contemplative practice. Next, in chapter seven, we will see how nothingness sheds some light on the hidden nature of contemplation. Finally, chapter eight will round out this little book with some reflections on prayer in secret.

One note: occasionally, I will invite you to "savor" some phrases or some instructions. For instance, savor the phrase, *just nothing*. I am inviting you to take it into your heart and pray over it, reflect on it, or just repeat it in your mind like a mantra. Quite simply, savoring a word, phrase, or instruction means to taste it. I am asking you to let a bit of spiritual wisdom go to work on you. In fact, savoring is like the second step of *lectio divina*: *meditatio*, that is, ruminating. Chew on it. Taste it and let God open new vistas on your practice of centering prayer through the word or phrase. Let God open you to the divine presence through it. These phrases will build toward a set of instructions at the very end of the book titled "Instruction Prayer for Deepening into Mystical Nothingness". Commentary will follow the instruction prayer. The purpose of this instruction prayer is to summarize the essential points of this little book and to offer you, the reader and practitioner, a tool for use with your own prayer. it is a prayer to read or say before or after your time of centering prayer.

Finally, I offer a disclaimer: this is a very different take on Christian contemplation. At least, it differs greatly from how many authors normally treat contemplation. I hope this little book not only offers you practical advice on centering prayer (or on any other contemplative practice), but also stretches you. I intend to break ideas about God, self, and the relation to God. In this, I am simply following the great parade of apophatic mystics down through the ages. Also, remember that this is but one way of approaching God and contemplation. it is not the only way or even the best way.

In reading this little book, you may notice a good deal of repetition. This is also a conscious decision. There are only a handful of insights contained here, which I intend to present in a number of ways. But, more deeply, we need repetition to help us savor and start to live truths that, at first glance, we may not wholly understand or which may not register. So, I encourage you to be patient with repeating themes and lines, and also to ingest the bits of wisdom on a deeper level when they do recur.

I hope these teachings help all spiritual seekers discover the joy of divine oneness, irrespective of religion, denomination, or lack thereof. May God's generous and gracious love be with all of you.

# A Brief Introduction to Centering Prayer

Whether you are new to contemplative practice and prayer or a seasoned veteran in the spiritual life, centering prayer is a practice of beautiful simplicity and vast depth that can help us receive the gift of God's own life - in short, contemplation. Christian tradition has always affirmed that contemplation is God's pure gift to us. We can only prepare to receive the gift. Centering prayer serves that preparation.

At one and the same time, centering prayer is a relationship with the God who is within us, and a discipline that fosters this incredible relationship. The whole purpose of centering prayer is to awaken us to the gift of contemplation, which is already given. For, we are always already one with God from the first moment of our existence. Contemplation involves allowing our oneness with God to become real for us. It is the full awakening to God's mystery in us and beyond us. As such, it means transcending our thinking, our feelings, our efforts, and our very existence. It is all about resting in God through interior silence and stillness.

Furthermore, centering prayer is fully Christian. One of the architects of centering prayer, Thomas Keating, tells us,

> [T]he source of Centering Prayer, as in all methods leading to Christian Contemplative Prayer, is the Indwelling Trinity: Father, Son, and Holy Spirit. The focus of centering prayer is the deepening of our relationship with the living Christ. It tends to

build communities of faith and bond the members together in mutual friendship and love.³

And, it does not replace any other type of prayer, whether it is the rosary or just talking to God.

Moreover, centering prayer is a way to implement Jesus' teaching on the inner room and secret prayer in the sixth chapter of the Gospel of Matthew: *But when you pray, go to your inner room, close the door, and pray to your Father in secret. And your Father who sees in secret will repay you (Matthew 6:6).*

For Jesus, secret prayer leads us into ever-deepening levels of silence. "Entering the inner room" means the silence of external noise. "Closing the door" means the silence of thinking and the internal dialogue. "Praying to our Father in secret" means sinking into the silence of self and the Silence of God. Jesus invites us to commune with God beyond all thought, feeling, experience, even being. Prayer in secret is secret from our thoughts, feelings, experiences, and our self-awareness.

The how: simply disregard all thoughts and sink into God. *Enter your inner room* by letting go of external stimuli and your ordinary level of psychological awareness - plans, feelings, thoughts. *Close the door* by letting go of your interior dialogue, your self-reflections, and even self-consciousness. And, *pray to your Abba in secret.* Let God be God in the silence. Sink into the divine nothingness. Uniquely, centering prayer emphasizes consent to God over concentration. To establish and renew this consent, you use a sacred word. For, while silent you will experience numerous thoughts. Handle all thoughts with a simple and deft spiritual

---

³ Keating, Thomas, *Open Mind, Open Heart: The Contemplative Dimension of the Gospel*, NY: Continuum, 2006, 176.

move: Whenever you become engaged with your thoughts, simply, promptly, and gently return to the sacred word.

Thomas Keating specifies the method of centering prayer by offering four guidelines. They help us by providing "directions" to secret prayer, preparing for contemplative prayer. These are guidelines, however, and not rules. Thus, they do not require slavish adherence. Rather, they lightly direct us in our prayer. So, do not worry about following the rules or doing the prayer wrong. There are (maybe) two possible ways not to do the prayer correctly: to think deliberately some thought and so break your intention or not to pray at all. Here are the four guidelines:

**The Guidelines of Centering Prayer[4]**

Guideline 1 - Choose a sacred word as the symbol of your intention to consent to God's presence and action within.

Guideline 2 - Sitting comfortably and with eyes closed, settle briefly and silently introduce the sacred word as the symbol of your consent to God's presence and action within.

Guideline 3 - When engaged with your thoughts, return ever-so-gently to the sacred word.

Guideline 4 - At the end of the prayer period, remain in silence with eyes close for a couple of minutes.

Let us examine each guideline. First, "Guideline 1 - Choose a sacred word as the symbol of your intention to consent to God's presence and action within." The sacred word symbolizes our intention to consent to God who dwells within us. But, it is not sacred because of its meaning. The

---

[4] *Ibid.*, 177-178

effortlessness. But, you may notice that thoughts will keep coming. Hence, there is a need for the third guideline. It is the heart of the instructions. The point of centering prayer is to enter into interior silence, mystical silence. And interior silence means detachment from our thoughts, from everything going on in our inner world. We sit in silence with pure faith, resting in God beyond thinking. Yet, what do we do with our thinking? We return to the sacred word, with gentleness, when we are engaged with our active thinking. We come back to the word when we are getting stuck in our thinking, when we are getting caught up in our self-talk.

The point is not to eliminate all thoughts. Rather, we pay no attention to our thoughts. We let them withdraw into the background. But, we do not oppose them. We let all our thoughts come into our minds. This prayer is not about concentration or attention, both of which imply personal and willful effort. Centering prayer is about effortlessness. It is about intention and consent - leading to self-surrender. So, having thoughts is not a problem. Thinking our thoughts during centering prayer is the issue. Thoughts become a problem when we purposely think them. We grow in our centering prayer when we are lose interest in and are detached from our thoughts, not when we have no thoughts at all.

Keating describes the word "thoughts" as an "umbrella term."[6] A thought is any perception at all: a physical feeling, outside sounds, reflections, ideas, internal pictures, emotional feelings, memories, self-talk, and even mystical experiences. Thoughts are a completely normal and totally unavoidable part of the experience of centering prayer. In fact they are a vital part of the healing process - some thoughts contain what needs to be healed.

---

[6] *Ibid.*, 178

word is sacred because it expresses our intention to consent. It a way of conveying, then renewing, your intention to open yourself to God and accept God as God is. Here are some examples of sacred words: God, Abba, Jesus, love, peace, silence, or joy. A religious word, though, is not necessary.

The sacred word can be any word, but Keating recommends a word of one or two syllables. The shorter the word, the better, for a longer word can stimulate thinking. Just so, a word that means a great deal to us can stimulate thinking. Still, there is not a magic word, or a special word that guarantees silence. No word is wrong, and no word is better than the other. Nevertheless, once you choose a sacred word, it is best not to change it during the period of centering prayer. If you do, again, that would be a step into thinking.

Second, "Guideline 2 - Sitting comfortably and with eyes closed, settle briefly and silently introduce the sacred word as the symbol of your consent to God's presence and action within." Before you begin your time of meditation, set up a good environment: a place and time of day that is quiet, an area in which you will not be interrupted easily, and a comfortable yet solid chair. Furthermore, let yourself get calm and quiet on the inside before you pray.

Sit comfortable, but not in a position that can lead to sleep. Keep your back straight, feet on the floor, and hands in your lap. Let your eyes close gently. Closing our eyes symbolizes letting go, letting go of the outside and inside worlds.[5] To start, say - on the inside - the sacred word. And, "say" it with gentleness. Our interior attitude is to be alert and open. Here is a slight warning: if you fall asleep, just continue praying when you wake up.

Third, "Guideline 3 - When engaged with your thoughts, return ever-so-gently to the sacred word." So, we begin by saying the sacred word within and with

---

[5] *Ibid.*, 178

Furthermore, the sacred word may become hazy or vanish all together. Constant repetition of the sacred is not the goal. We use the word when we need it: to reestablish our intention to consent to God dwelling within us. Otherwise, if we are silent within and not paying attention to our thoughts there is no need for the word.

Keating has this important advice: Our attitude towards thoughts, rather, is to accept them and let them go in one fluid motion - without resistance, without holding on to them, and without reacting to them.[7] But, if you get caught in them, ever-so-gently return to your sacred word. "Resist no thought, retain no thought, react emotionally to no thought,"[8] but when you do engage your thoughts, return ever-so-gently to the sacred word.

Some other preliminary instructions: don't judge your experience of centering prayer. Disregard all experiences. Just let all thoughts come and go without expectation or judgment. If you get annoyed with yourself, let this slide, too. A highly charged emotion can tempt us into thinking. But even when this does happen, return to your word with gentleness. And, return promptly. To renew our consent to God by returning to the sacred word, with the utmost gentleness, means we choose God over self. It means we are loving God. And it is the only thing we do. We are entering into God's way of communicating: silence. "Keep in mind that God's first language is silence."[9]

Additionally, even the thought that we are not thinking is a thought. It's a very subtle thought, but a thought nonetheless. In centering prayer we head towards a state of non-thinking silence, detached from all thoughts - even self-reflections. "The method of centering prayer is designed to

---

[7] *Ibid.*, 129
[8] *Ibid.*, 127
[9] *Ibid.*, 48

turn off the ordinary flow of thoughts that reinforces our habitual way of thinking of ourselves and of looking at the world."[10]

Just stay put. Stay in the silence when you feel bored, irritated, fidgety, and hopelessly impatient. Wait there and let all these feelings, all thoughts, pass. Everything passes. All thoughts will pass, just let them.

Fourth, "Guideline 4 - At the end of the prayer period, remain in silence with eyes closed for a couple of minutes." Remaining in silence for a few minutes allows for a transition. This enables us to bring the interior silence into our daily life. Practically, to create a discipline of centering prayer, do it twice a day for twenty minutes each time. Typically, it is best to have one period in the morning and the other in the late afternoon or early evening.

Centering prayer pivots on the twin attitudes of pure faith and letting go. Pure faith means unknowing, knowing beyond the mind by knowing nothing. Pure faith is essential because we cannot know God directly with our minds. We have to submit to the darkness of faith, and it is darkness because all the abilities of our minds cannot come close to grasping who God is. Rather, we accept God as God is by pure faith. So, even when we have no experience of God, no spiritual feelings, trust God. Trust God no matter what - even beyond your experience. Surrender to God without restraints.

Letting go works with pure faith, for letting go means dropping all the ways we want to use our minds to experience God. Letting go is an effortless action. We simply let every thought come, and, at the same time, let every thought keep going. And when attractive and repulsive thoughts snag us, we return ever-so-gently to our sacred word. But, often, letting go will be experienced as just putting up with

---

[10] *Ibid.*, 120

everything going on in our heads. No matter what it is, no matter how long it takes, it will pass. Every thought and perception will pass.

Furthermore, an experience of God is a thought, it is not God. No experience of God is as important as God. God does not want to be loved for how God makes us feel. No one does, least of all God. So, in centering prayer, we let go of all thoughts. We, especially, let go of spiritual thoughts, of thoughts about God. No thought is as important as interior silence. Centering prayer is a time for a most intimate self-denial: a denial or, rather, a letting go, of who we think we are, of our thoughts and feelings.[11] Keating notes:

> Letting go and not reflecting on what you are doing is the correct way to conduct yourself in this prayer. The method doesn't consist in how you sit or in the length of time you give, but in how you handle the thoughts that arise.[12]

The discipline of centering prayer is doing it twice a day for twenty minutes each time. Most practice one period in the morning and one in the late afternoon or early evening. In this way, you receive some stability in your day life through a balanced access to interior silence. This is a practice that refreshes on a deep level - beyond thinking, feelings, and your very self.

So, simply remain in silence, disregarding all thoughts, and resting in God in pure faith. Just let God love you. It is simple loving attentiveness to God beyond all thought. Withdraw your attention from the ordinary flow of thoughts in your mind. Be interiorly still and quiet and allow your divine identity to surface.

---

[11] *Ibid.*, 124
[12] *Ibid.*, 87

*What Centering Prayer is and what it is not*[13]

1. It is not a technique but a way of cultivating a relationship with God.
2. It is not a relaxation exercise but it may be refreshing.
3. It is not a form of self-hypnosis but a way to quiet the mind while maintaining its alertness.
4. It is not a charismatic gift but a path of transformation.
5. It is not a para-psychological experience but an exercise of faith, hope, and selfless love.
6. It is not limited to the "felt presence" of God but is rather a deepening of faith in God's abiding Presence.
7. It is not reflective or spontaneous prayer, but simply resting in God.

---

[13] *Ibid.,* 181

# Chapter 1

# Why Nothing?

So, why nothing? Why offer this teaching? I ask because it may seem, at the very least, like nothingness is an unusual topic for a Christian, maybe even bordering on heretical. I hope to show you, however, that nothingness is essential to the contemplative dimension of the Gospel and, hence, to Christianity. According to the Christian apophatic mystics, the secret of Christianity - and the secret of contemplation - is *nothing*. In fact, nothingness lines up one-hundred percent with the way of Jesus presented in the New Testament. Of course, it may feel new to call the way of Jesus a way of "nothingness." It may feel like a startling, provocative, or just plain confusing way of describing the path of the Gospel. It is, however, rooted in Christian tradition. Indeed, the teachings of Jesus support it. To make some sense of nothingness, allow me to offer five reasons for presenting this teaching.

First, nothingness is at the center of centering prayer, the deepening of centering prayer into contemplation, and the unfolding of contemplation into oneness with God. Nothingness provides some very key insights for our practice of centering prayer: for how we handle our thoughts and allow our consent to become divine surrender. As centering prayer deepens into contemplation, nothingness helps us both see our role and navigate the difficulties that arise. Then, nothingness gives us some hints about what divine oneness may look like, and even what it is. In short, nothingness is a contemplative path, a path to happiness.

Second, nothingness, as I have already briefly alluded to, has a tradition in Christianity. I will discuss this tradition more fully in the following chapter, but I will offer a few points here. Talking about nothingness may seem, well, nihilistic - as in bordering on the hopelessness of a total absence of ultimate meaning, and, thus, God. *Christian* nothingness, however, turns out to be very positive and meaningful. The Christian apophatic mystics teach that we need nothing to be happy. We do not need to do anything or be anyone to enjoy unlimited bliss right now. We can be happy with nothing.

Moreover, for the Christian apophatic mystics, God is nothing. This does not mean that there is no God or that God does not exist. Quite the opposite. Nothingness affirms and safeguards divine transcendence and mystery. Christian apophatic mystics are keenly aware that God will always elude our language, our images, and our thoughts. Rather starkly, divine nothingness reminds us that God transcends everything. Indeed, because these same mystics resolutely avow our oneness with God, nothingness also protects the mystery at the core of the human person and of creation in general. We have a depth of incomprehensible mystery that no psychology, sociology, or even theology can ever exhaust.

Christian apophatic mysticism, however, is not limited to specific uses of the word "nothing". Words like emptiness, silence, stillness, desert, desolate, unknowing, and incomprehensible and the very method of denying all names ascribed to God all "point" to nothingness. They all function as nothingness does: they free us from thinking and language to open to God as God really is and not as we *think* God is.

Third, nothingness means the transcendence of being. God as God transcends existence: this is how mysterious and incomprehensible God really is. Thus, our contemplative practice must also transcend being to realize divine oneness. Being is too "thingy." *To be* is *to be known*: what exists is knowable and graspable by the human mind. This principle underlies apophatic mysticism: being is thinking. Thinking always intends being. Being is the object of thought. They are identical because thinking always concerns some being and being remains the "what" of thinking, it is what thought thinks.

> [T]hought is always the apprehension of some being. For whatever is thought is necessarily thought as something, i.e. as some being...that which is not, cannot be thought, for to think absolute non-being would be to have no object or content for thought, to be not thinking anything, and hence not to be thinking.[14]

Being and thinking are identical. Being is thinking. Thus, when we let go of thinking in centering prayer we also let go of being. We enter into nothingness. Nothingness transcends being and therefore thinking, too.

Furthermore, contemplative teachers often assert that the essence of practice is just *to be* – as in just being *to* God. When we say that, however, we allow for a subtle duality: *my* being is present to *God's* Being. There are still two beings. Being is a particular substance. In this case (contemplative prayer), my particular substance is attending to God's particular substance. This respects neither divine nor human mystery. The human person is more than a substance just as God is more than a substance (more on this in the next chapter). When one is "just being" one is still separate from God. Nothingness transcends this separation precisely because "it" is not a thing or a particular substance at all. In

---

[14] Perl, Eric David, *Theophany: The Neoplatonic Philosophy of Dionysius the Areopagite*, Albany, NY: State University of New York Press, 2007. Kindle Edition, ch.1.

fact, I will claim in chapter four that nothingness is a suitable Christian term for nonduality. For the Christian apophatic mystics, nothingness means that at the deepest level of reality we are the same as God even though we are our own distinct persons. Because "just being" implies subtle separation, we must let it go in our contemplative practice. For our centering prayer to be truly apophatic we are invited to let go thinking, feeling, experience, self-consciousness, and even being. Surrender being and allow nothingness.

Fourth, nothingness reveals the radical nature of love. Nothingness gives us a glimpse of just how wild and unreserved divine love is. God loves for nothing, for no reason at all, out of sheer gratuity. Love is utterly gratuitous. Love is from and for nothing. Love loves simply because love is love. It is pure gift and, therefore, based on nothing. Nothingness, then, is sheer gratuity; and sheer gratuity is love.

This is evident in the doctrine of the Trinity, which proclaims God as self-emptying love. As self-emptying or self-giving love, God empties God-self absolutely. Abba empties out in ecstatically giving the divine Self away to the Son, who then gratuitously surrenders back to the Abba - and, this flux of perfect self-surrender is the Holy Spirit. This love is totally for the other, and, hence, empty in and of itself. So, God is absolute emptiness or nothingness precisely as self-giving love. Divine nothingness is gratuitous love loving for no reason at all. This is the *agape* of the Gospels: the love Jesus teaches and enacts. In fact, from of old the Church has said that this is the love with which we love God. Nothingness shows us how to love, for there is nothing we can do to earn this love.

Fifth, I offer this teaching on nothingness because I believe it is an insight God gave me. Once, while centering during an eight-day intensive centering prayer retreat, an insight passed through my mind: "just nothing." Being obedient to the practice, I let that thought go. But, it came back to me again and again - in and out of the meditation. In fact, the insight stayed with me over the course of the retreat, deepening my practice and my vision of centering prayer and Christian contemplative living. It has stayed with me ever since. I believe it to be divine inspiration that the way and "goal" of contemplative prayer is nothing. Simply put, I offer this teaching on nothingness because I believe it is a gift from God meant to help us grow spiritually.

I conclude this chapter by offering a summary and, hopefully, a clarification. Following Thomas Keating's useful approach, let us looking at what the nothingness is and what it is not:

Nothingness is:
1. A pointer to the incomprehensible mystery of God
2. A pointer to the incomprehensible mystery of the human person who is one with God
3. Based in the Christian tradition
4. A way of practicing centering prayer beyond all symbols, methods, and "just being"
5. A way to understand God's gratuitous love

Nothingness is not:
1. Saying there is no God
2. Just an experience or a feeling
3. A technique for acquiring or achieving pure contemplation
4. Saying it is the ONLY way to follow Christ or understand divine love
5. The only way to practice centering prayer

# Chapter 2

# The Christian Tradition of Nothingness

*God is Nothing*

Centering Prayer emerges from a distinct tradition within Christianity: apophatic mysticism. Christian apophatic mysticism, in my view, is made up of theology, how we understand God, and practice, a spiritual path and approach to the practice of living the Gospel. In this chapter I will flesh out these two parts of Christian apophatic mysticism under the topics "God is nothing" and "The path of nothingness." In each section I will incorporate the different insights of mystics from Christian history. The point of this chapter is to show the specifically *Christian* nature of nothingness.

I summarize Christian apophatic mysticism in the following manner: *God is nothing; therefore, the path to God is nothingness.* Here, we will tackle nothingness as an apophatic way of un-naming God, a theological language. It is called "apophasis," which means "no image" or "unsaying." Apophasis recognizes that to write "God" is to create an idol, for language attempts to grasp God by a concept. To write "God" is to make God into an object. Apophasis recognizes our language about God will always fail. But, it rests on its twin, kataphasis, or "saying." Kataphasis is the world of images, symbols, and names the Bible and theology use to describe God. So, God is life. God is light. God is love. This is all kataphasis. Apophasis builds on kataphasis, our words for God give way to their unsaying. Hence, apophasis is a language of unsaying. But, it is not just saying God is beyond language or thinking. For, even to say "God is inexpressible" is to express something about God! So apophasis is constantly correcting itself, thus it is never a closed language. It never rests on a conclusion or a final statement. Apophatic mystics develop this unsaying with a wide range of negative metaphors: darkness, silence, emptiness, and, of course, nothing.

Apophasis, moreover, is a very biblical enterprise. It rigorously adheres to the first commandment: "I am the LORD your God, who brought you out of the land of Egypt, out of the house of slavery. You shall not have other gods beside me. You shall not make for yourself an idol"(Exodus 20:2-4). Our most unrecognized idols are our concepts. These can be the most deceptive idols. We easily believe that concepts tell us something definitive about God, which we then interpret through our own set of personal, social, psychological, cultural, and, especially, egoic lenses.

Nothingness, however, is not a final name of God, but a destabilizing of all names, all ideas, all thinking that rests on names for God – a radical denial of all them, yes, but only after we have affirmed them. So, apophasis is in relationship with kataphasis. At this point in the history of Christianity, I think we have reached a saturation of divine names, theologies, and ideas about God. It is time for a radical apophasis.

Apophasis, though, is not just a theological language game; it rests on the life of Jesus. For, the origin of Christianity is Jesus' intimacy with God as Abba, but also as nothing - Abba connotes how Jesus experienced God as unmerited mercy, tender, and loving. Yet, we forget that Jesus also knew God as transcendent mystery. For, Jesus often prays in the desert, in solitude, during the night. And, it seems all his glorious experiences of God (such as his baptism and the transfiguration) were for the benefit of those people around him (John the Baptist, the apostles). We can interpret the desert, solitude, and night as biblical symbols for nothingness. These images are significant pointers towards God as mystery, as the nothingness beyond experience and existence. God is nothing precisely because God is utterly beyond, unimaginably transcendent. God, for Jesus, is too real for existence and being. So, while God is our unconditionally loving Abba, God is also apophatic nothingness for Jesus. The Spirit transmits Jesus' intimacy with God to us down through the ages: being one with the Loving Nihil (Latin for "nothing") we call God.

Moreover, we can understand the cross as fundamental for the claim that God is nothing. Crucified, Jesus perceives no God at all. There is nothing. Thus, I suggest that Christ Crucified reveals God as nothing. The Gospel of Mark records the death of Jesus on the cross:

> At noon darkness came over the whole land until three in the afternoon. And at three o'clock Jesus cried out in a loud voice, "Eloi, Eloi, lema sabachthani?" which is translated, "My God, my God, why have you forsaken me?"...Jesus gave a loud cry and breathed his last.(Mk.15:33-37).

The cross negates divine being. Interpreting the event of the cross from the perspective of apophasis, Beverly Lanzetta says Christ Crucified reveals the negation of God:

> In breaking through the emptiness above his divine name, Christ reveals a God of unnaming, a God who subverts God's names. Death on the cross *is* the Absolute Unsaying, and therefore an Apophatic God, a God who frees us from God...this God who

is not God offers Godself and lays the mystery bare.[15]

In the same movement, Christ Crucified reveals God as nothing. The ultimate negation of the cross is the negation of divine being. The crucified God tells us that God is not what we think God is or even *that God is*. The crucified God reverses and overturns our notion of existence. Christ's death on the cross reveals God as the *nothing beyond all divnity* and this means that God-as-God transcends existence. Jesus Christ Crucified reveals God as the nothingness that transcends existence: beyond being and before being. Here, divine nothingness equals God as absolute mystery, outside our control, knowledge, and being. This is an essential message of the cross. Jesus Christ crucified reveals that God exceeds being. Christ crucified proclaims that being cannot contain God.

The crucifixion is the negation of God, the point of absolute negation, and the focus of all negativity. There is no such "thing" as God: only nothing. All our notions of God are crucified on the cross. Divine being is crucified and gives way to divine nothingness. Jesus crucified reveals God as the divine nothing, the *nihil* who surpasses existence itself yet submits to the vicissitudes of history out of concrete love for creation.

Along with the crucified, the Christian apophatic mystics have "unsaid" God through nothingness. In his twenty-third sermon, Meister Eckhart (a fourteenth-century German Dominican friar) probes into four usual names for God: goodness, being, truth, and one. He says none of them apply to God. He continues: "But if God is neither goodness

---

[15] Lanzetta, Beverly, *The Other Side of Nothingness: Toward a Theology of Radical Openness*, Albany, NY: State University of New York Press, 2001, 88-89.

nor being nor truth nor one, what then is He? He is pure nothing; he is neither this nor that."[16] For Eckhart, God is nothing. This is not an atypical statement among Christian apophatic mystics. Dionysius the pseudo-Areopagite, John Scottus Eriugena, even Thomas Merton all say this. The phrase has a number of levels of meaning. Let us inquire into five of them.

First, God transcends our understanding, perception, categories: God as no-thing. Henry Suso (another fourteenth-century German Dominican) typifies Christian apophatic mystics when he says God is "the nothing of all things." He also declares, "This nothing is called by common agreement 'God' and is in itself a something existing to an incomparable degree."[17] So, even though God is nothing, God is not an illusion but "a something existing to an incomparable degree." God is real. But, then Suso goes on to say the following:

> [O]ne cannot talk about it in the sense that one talks about a thing that can be clarified with words. Whatever one says about it describes not the least little bit what it is, no matter how many theologians and books there might be. To say that this nothing is intellect or being or fulfillment is certainly true according to what anyone can tell us about it. However, in true point of fact it is as far and farther from these things than if one were to call a fine pearl a chopping block.[18]

---

[16] *The Complete Mystical Works of Meister Eckhart*, trans. Maurice O'C. Walshe, revised by Bernard McGinn, NY: Crossroad, 2009, 287.

[17] *Henry Suso: The Exemplar with Two German Sermons*, trans. And ed. Frank Tobin, NY: Paulist Press, 1989, 319.

[18] *Ibid.*

All names for God are invalid because God transcends all of them. They may reflect an aspect of God's mystery, but the divine mystery will always elude all words. As Pseudo-Dionysius the Areopgaite says, "God is not known, not spoken, not named, not something among beings. God is All in all, Nothing in none, known to all in reference to all, and known to no one in reference to nothing."[19] God is not a thing in our world of things and beings.

God is so unknown that, according to John Scottus Eriugena, God does not know God's own self! He asks the following in his monumental work, *On The Division of Nature*: "How…can the divine nature understand of itself what it is, seeing that it is nothing (*nihil*)? For it surpasses everything that is, since it is not even being but all being derives from it, and by virtue of its excellence it is supereminent over every essence and every substance."[20] So, God not only transcends creatures and the human mind. God also transcends being.

Thus, second, God transcends existence. God transcends existence precisely because God creates all that is. Divine mystery cannot even be captured by existence. To exist literally means to "stand out." God does not seem to "stand out" at all, but remains hidden in mystery – absolutely incomprehensible as much as absolutely available. And, as I said earlier, to be is to be known: what exists is knowable and graspable by the human mind. In Letter 1, Pseudo-Dionysius says this:

---

[19] *The Divine Names and The Mystical Theology*, trans. John D. Jones, Milwaukee, WI: Marquette University Press, 1999, 179.
[20] John Scotus Eriugena, *Periphyseon*, quoted in Donald Duclow, "Divine Nothingness and Self-Creation in John Scotus Eriugena," *The Journal of Religion*, Vol.57, Number 2, April 1977, 111.

> [God] himself solidly transcends mind and being. He is completely unknown and non-existent. He exists beyond being and he is known beyond the mind. And this quite positively complete unknowing is knowledge of him who is above everything that is known.[21]

Commenting on Pseudo-Dionysius, John Jones says the following about God:

> Beyond all, the divinity is not a supreme essence or being beyond all other things. Beyond all, the divinity is not the ultimate source or cause of all that is. Beyond all [the] divinity: nothing...beyond source and beyond cause...Beyond all: not a supreme being which is be-ing in itself apart from all other beings; beyond all: nothing...We must not understand nothing simply as no-thing or no-being, so that we understand nothing as be-ing itself,...or as simply and unlimitedly be-ing. Rather, nothing: beyond be-ing and hence, beyond cause.[22]

God is not the Supreme Being we normally envision God to be. To say God is being is to say God is a being, even if the most supreme of beings. We have God as a thing again - a powerful thing, but still a being or thing amid the world of beings or things. Christian apophatic mystics will say, instead, God does not exist. God is too real merely to exist. Things exist. People exist. God is the very ground of

---

[21] *Pseudo-Dionysius: The Complete Works*, trans. Colm Luibheid, NY: Paulist Press, 1987, 263.
[22] Jones, John D., "Introduction," *The Divine Names and the Mystical Theology*, 90-91

existence. As such, God does not, strictly speaking, exist: God is nothing. Though very real, and not an illusion, being does not contain God.

Third, nothingness is the unsaying of God. Rather directly, Meister Eckhart quotes Pseudo-Dionysius saying the following: "Dionysius says: God is nothing. By this he means that God is incomprehensible as Nothing. God is super-essential, super-rational, super-intelligible."[23] Eckhart is getting at more than just affirming divine mystery. The phrase "God is nothing" unsays God. It deconstructs our usual ideas about God, even God's transcendence (God as beyond our words, our minds, even being). It is a language strategy that serves both to shock people out of and help people see their substantialist understanding of God (substantialist means "as a substance or as a being"). We have a substantialist understanding of God whenever we attempt to say God, to write God, to put God into our language, or to think God, and stop there. This is simply the function of language: trying to express in words the divinity beyond being. We cannot refer to God with language and to attempt to do so is to lock the divine into categories of meaning and reified concepts that leave God-as-God behind. When we say "God" we all assume we know what we're talking about. Stop it. No one does.

The apophatic mystic knows that language and thought shape experience. What we think and say about God structures how we meet God. Language and thinking can be very limiting of God and us - our God concept can limit God's action in our lives as well as reduce God to some*thing* we can understand and use to confirm our agendas, to authorize our opinions and views. Basically, God becomes the ultimate validation for our egos! This leads to believing

---

[23] *The Wisdom of Meister Eckhart*, ed. Jan Stryz, New Grail Publishing: St. Paul, MN, 2003, 23.

in a God of experiences, of thoughts and feelings, to a God who is an object. The very act of writing "God" limits God and can easily become idolatry.

For instance, when we speak about God as a person we develop subconscious expectations and assumptions regarding this God – that this God exists as we do, is separate from us, and must act as we presume a good person does. Can you see how this imprisons God? This subtle idolatry winds up treating God as an object: in fact all our loves can be objectifying, whether love for God, others, ourselves, or creation. God is not an object outside us to be experienced on our terms. Language and thinking attempt to grasp God and bring God into our territory. When we treat God as an object we make God into some*thing* we can *experience* on *our* terms.

Even to call God "ineffable" or "mystery" still submits to the structures of thinking and language. Once we say God is ineffable, we have to correct it by saying "God is beyond ineffable." But then that statement needs correction: God is beyond "beyond ineffable." So, there is an infinite regress and correction of the last statement. God always eludes the final statement. There is never a conclusion the mind can grasp.

So, as a statement, "God is nothing" still locks the divine into substantialist categories. "God is nothing" locks the nonentified divinity (non-entified means "not an entity"), the nonsubstantialist divinity (nonsubstantialist means "not a substance") - the nothing - into substance and being categories. The very structure of language makes nothing into something, into being and substance.

However, the force of "nothing" unsays and subverts these very substantialist linguistic structures. To say "God is nothing" is to unsay. It is a paradox. For, calling anything "nothing" is meaningless to our rational minds. "Nothing" has no meaning, no being, it means - literally - *nothing*! Here is the point: God is not a thing for us to name, nor does God exist as we presume existence to be. Further, the phrase, "God is nothing," shatters the infinite regress or, maybe, encapsulates the infinite regress because "nothing" is a meaningless word at bottom. Nothing is nothing. It is equivalent to the infinite regress. God is nothing: beyond being, beyond nothing, beyond beyond, nothing as nothing in nothing through nothing beyond nothing. Therefore, "God is nothing" is a supremely apophatic statement that is paradoxically both substantialist and nonsubstantialist.

Nothingness undoes all reference to the divine. Perhaps this is best signified by no signification? Divine nothingness may be signified best with no symbol, but only a blankness, by a blank and empty space, a linguistic desert: Even though it still keeps God in language, nothingness can liberate God from substance and the structures of language, and hence of thought. For, these keep God locked into being, making God out to be *something, a* being - *to be* at all.

Fourth, nothingness simultaneously denies and transcends all opposites, all duality, even that between creature and Creator. Nothingness is not simply the opposite of being. The nothing reconciles the opposites of existence and non-existence by transcending being and non-being. Indeed, nothingness reconciles the duality of creator and creature. Christian apophatic mystics are the ones who often remind us of God's incredible closeness, of God's oneness with us to the point of being our deepest identity.

In sermon 71, Eckhart unpacks a single sentence from the Book of Acts, "Paul rose from the ground and with eyes open he saw nothing"(Acts 9:8). He says:

> It seems to me that this little word [*i.e., nothing*] has four meanings. One meaning is: When he got up from the ground, with eyes open he saw nothing, and the nothing was God; for when he saw God, he

[Luke] calls this a nothing. The second: When he got up he saw nothing but God. The third: In all things he saw nothing but God. The fourth: When he saw God, he viewed all things as nothing.[24]

Eckhart proposes four meanings of "nothing": 1) the nothing was God, 2) he saw nothing but God, 3) In all things he saw nothing but God, 4) When he saw God, he viewed all things as nothing. In other words: God is nothing, there is only God, all things are the nothing, and without God everything is not (does not exist).

Eckhart is saying that God transcends being and is not a thing of this world. Thus, God is all things. To say God is nothing is to say God is all. In sermon 40 Eckhart says, "All creatures are a pure nothing."[25] All things are *the* pure nothing, the divine nothing. The ultimate identity and reality of every creature is the nothing. All that exists is a manifestation of the transcendent nothing. Every creature is distinct from God, but each one is also identical with God. So, the nothing signifies absolutely transcendent mystery and incomprehensible oneness with all that is: the oneness of the exact same identity.

Fifth, nothingness is nothingness. In the end, nothing is just that, nothing! Pseudo-Dionysius says, in his *Divine Names*, that the divinity "is cause of all, but itself: nothing" - just nothing, nothing as nothing.[26] Nothing as nothing means there can be no thought or reflection on the "nature" of nothingness. It is not to be thought out or reflected on. Nothing, beyond the concept, is quite simply nothing. Thus, do not try to describe or define nothingness. That is not the

---

[24] *Meister Eckhart: Teacher and Preacher*, ed. Bernard McGinn, NY: Paulist Press, 1986, 320.
[25] *Ibid.*, 250
[26] *The Divine Names and the Mystical Theology*, 113

goal. Rather, let go of all talk, thoughts, comments, and agendas to awaken to the nothing.

Nothingness radicalizes the Absolute Mystery of God. Nothing: beyond being, beyond "beyond being," beyond omnipotence, beyond all beyonds, below being, behind being, beyond non-being, not non-being, beyond all nots, beyond nothing. Thus, we cannot experience nothing. Nothingness belongs to the realm of non-experience, which is true of God. We may always experience *something*, but *nothingness* transcends our experience. This points to God as radically transcendent mystery and leaves us without anything to cling to. Without clinging to anything we begin to see the divine in all things. Angelus Silesius, a seventeenth-century German mystic, puts in a poetic fashion:

*The Godhead Is A Naught*
The tender Godhead is a naught and more than naught;
Who sees nothing in all, believe me, he sees God.[27]

We do not rely on anything to encounter God. We rely on no word, name, thought, feeling, or experience of the divine. We simply open to the divine. We rest in nothing. This is the point – follow the path of nothingness into *the* nothing.

*The Path of Nothingness*

Since God is nothing, the path to God is nothingness. Scholars often discuss the theological aspect of apophatic mysticism, but can forget nothingness as a spiritual path. I speak about the theology of nothingness to get you on the path of nothingness, to help you realize oneness with the

---

[27] Angelus Silesius, *The Cherubinic Wanderer*, NY: Paulist Press, 1986, 44.

nothing. As a path, nothingness is contemplation itself, our practice of contemplation, what must happen in us, through us, and to us. The realization of our own nothingness is the realization of oneness with God.

When we examine the prayer life and the teachings of Jesus, it is very reasonable to describe both as "nothing." First, let us turn to Jesus' prayer life. Recall that most of Jesus' prayer took place in solitary locales: the desert, deserted places, mountain tops. The desert and solitary places symbolize nothingness – divine nothingness and interior nothingness. We can find examples of Jesus praying with words and feelings in the presence of others, but more often we have these moments of solitude. Frances Kelly Nemeck and Marie Theresa Coombs reflect on the prayer life of Jesus: "What do you suppose Jesus *did* during his solitary prayer? What do you suppose he *said* or *thought* while praying? He did *nada* during his solitary prayer. Jesus said nothing and thought nothing while praying."[28] Jesus' prayer was composed of nothing; his prayer was non-thinking nothingness. Nemeck and Coombs go on to say, "What could he do that he was not already doing? What word (audible or mental) could he say or think that would not be superfluous—he is the Word of the Father, incarnate."[29] While his prayer life had moments of words, feelings, and thoughts – as all prayer lives do – his anchor, it seems, was nothingness: wordless, non-thinking, and beyond experience.

Furthermore, the plethora of Jesus' teachings on letting go, self-denial, losing oneself, humility, detachment, and kenosis, can all be described as "nothingness." In Mark 8:34-35 Jesus says: "Whoever wishes to come after me must deny himself, take up his cross, and follow me. For whoever

---

[28] Nemeck, Frances Kelly, and Coombs, Marie Theresa, *Contemplation*, Eugene, OR: Wipf and Stock, 1982, 33.
[29] *Ibid.*, 33-34

wishes to save his life will lose it, but whoever loses his life for my sake and that of the gospel will save it." This is clear teaching on nothingness, the nothingness of self, and that we must deny or let go or annihilate the self. Thomas Keating even has his own translation of losing oneself from Matthew's Gospel. He translates Matthew 10:39 as the "One who brings himself to nought for me discovers who he is."[30] Nothingness is an alternate term for self-denial. It is not the only term, but a suitable one that builds immediate connections with apophatic theology. Here are some more examples of Jesus' teaching on nothingness:

> If your hand causes you to sin, cut it off. (Mark 9:43)
> 
> Whoever does not accept the kingdom of God like a child will not enter it. (Mark 10:15)
> 
> Go, sell what you have, and give to (the) poor and you will have treasure in heaven; then come, follow me. (Mark 10:21)
> 
> Take nothing for the journey...(Luke 9:3)
> 
> The one who is least among all of you is the one who is the greatest. (Luke 9:48)
> 
> The Son of Man has nowhere to rest his head. (Luke 9:58)

---

[30] Keating, Thomas, *Manifesting God*, NY: Lantern Books, 2005, 93.

Everyone who humbles himself will be exalted, but the one who exalt himself will be humbled. (Luke 14:11)

If any one comes to me without hating his father and mother, wife and children, brothers and sisters, and even his own life, he cannot be my disciple. Whoever does not carry his own cross and come after me cannot be my disciple. (Luke 14:26-27)

Everyone of you who does not renounce all his possessions cannot be my disciple. (Luke 14:33)

Blessed are the poor in spirit, theirs is the kingdom of heaven. (Matthew 5:3)

All these teachings are about letting go, self-emptying. Sometimes they regard a specific object of detachment. Often they are general invitations to let ourselves become nothing and so discover who we really are. Traditional names for the nothingness are "spiritual poverty" and the "way of the cross." And, here, we could include all the sayings from the letters of St. Paul about dying with Christ and being crucified with Christ. It is the same process as allowing nothingness in prayer and in daily life.

I will simply note it here, but Jesus' teaching on prayer in Matthew 6:6 also falls into the category of teachings on nothingness: "If you want to pray, enter your inner room, close the door, and pray to your Father in secret, and your Father who is in secret will reward you." Prayer in secret is the prayer of nothingness, which we will discuss in chapter eight.

In addition to the prayer life and teachings of Jesus, Christian apophatic tradition has often called contemplative prayer, unknowing, letting go, and detachment, "nothingness." Many mystics have referred to letting go of all obstacles to divine love, emptying oneself before God, detachment, humility, and prayer – specifically contemplative prayer – as following a path of nothingness and as just plain nothing. Thomas Keating himself makes this reference in *Manifesting God* when he states: "The contemplative dimension of the Gospel is Christ's program for getting acquainted with the Ultimate Reality as it really is, which is 'no thing.' 'No thing' means no particular thing, whether concept, feeling, or bodily experience."[31]

Three apophatic mystics represent the tradition well: the author of *The Cloud of Unknowing*, John of the Cross, and Meister Eckhart. Practitioners of centering prayer will recognize that both the author of *The Cloud* and John of the Cross are major sources for the method and spirituality of the prayer practice. Meister Eckhart only intensifies their insights. Savor each one, for they all describe detachment or letting go as nothingness, contemplation as nothingness, and even refer to self and God as nothing.

First, let us look at *The Cloud of Unknowing*. In chapter 68, the anonymous author of this fourteenth-century English mystical treatise forthrightly explains why contemplative prayer can be called "nothing":

> [D]uring contemplative prayer, your body's five senses and your soul's powers will think that you are doing nothing because they find nothing to feed on, but don't let that stop you - keep on working at this "nothing," as long as you are doing it for God's love. Persevere in contemplation with a renewed longing in your will to have God, remembering that your intellect cannot possess him. For I would rather be nowhere physically, wrestling with this

---

[31] Keating, *Manifesting God*, 2

obscure nothing, than be a powerful, rich lord, able to go wherever I want, whenever I want, always amusing myself with every "something" I own.[32]

The anonymous author prefers nothingness over all the somethings of the world, and is quite honest about our senses and our minds feeling like contemplation is nothing. Yet, he says to keep at the nothing, the nowhere, of contemplation. In fact, he feels it is better than a rich man's power and wealth. Indeed, the author is assured of the nothing because our intellect cannot possess God. He reminds us, though, to remain in the nothing out of love for God.

Following this, the author exhorts the reader: "abandon the world's 'everywhere' and 'something' in exchange for this infinitely more valuable nowhere and nothing."[33] The nowhere and the nothing are of infinite value! Abandon all everywhere and all something to open to the nothing. In the next chapter, 69, he says why we ought to be at home in nothingness: "Experiencing this nothing in its nowhere miraculously transforms a person's soul, outlook, and capacity for love."[34] The nothingness transforms us, but "it" is not "something" we can pin down with our minds: "[T]hink what you want of this nothingness. Regardless, you'll always find that it's a cloud of unknowing between you and God."[35] The author even identifies the nothingness as "the cloud of unknowing." Without thinking about it, *The Cloud* author wants us to love God in the nothingness: "So work diligently in this nothing, which is nowhere."[36]

---

[32] Anonymous, *The Cloud of Unknowing*, Brewster, Mass.: Paraclete Press, 2006. Kindle Edition, ch.68.
[33] *Ibid.*
[34] *Ibid.*, ch.69
[35] *Ibid.*
[36] *Ibid.*, ch.70

Next, consider John of the Cross. Before beginning his masterful work, *The Ascent of Mount Carmel*, John presents a sketch of Mount Carmel. This sketch summarizes his spiritual teaching. The "mount" symbolizes union with God. On either side of this mount are things, the "goods of heaven" and the "goods of earth": glory, joy, knowledge, possessions, consolation, rest. John describes attachment to these goods as "the way of the imperfect spirit." Right down the middle, leading up to the mount, John writes "The path of Mount Carmel the perfect spirit." And this path is "nothing, nothing, nothing, nothing, nothing, nothing, and even on the Mount nothing."[37] Extraordinary! John sums up the whole path of the perfect spirit in one word, "nothing." Even the top of the mount, divine union, is nothing. I will explore nothingness as oneness with God in chapter eight. For now, I will unpack the path of the perfect spirit.

In *The Ascent of Mount Carmel*, John describes what he means by the path of the perfect spirit as the path of nothing. He writes some couplets about it:

> To reach satisfaction in all
> Desire satisfaction in nothing.
> To come to possess all
> Desire the possession of nothing.
> To arrive at being all
> Desire to be nothing.
> To come to the knowledge of all
> Desire the knowledge of nothing.[38]

---

[37] *The Collected Works of St. John of the Cross*, trans. Kieran Kavanaugh and Otilio Rodriguez, Washington, DC: ICS Publications, 1991, 111.
[38] *Ibid.*, 150

Be satisfied with nothing. Possess nothing. Know nothing. In fact, be nothing! All satisfaction, possessions, knowledge, and even being can get between God and us. Our desire for them separates and causes us to treat them as gods in and of themselves. There is nothing wrong with satisfaction in all, possessing all, being all, and knowing all. But, the way to all is, paradoxically, nothing. In other words, be content with nothingness and let go of all things. John expresses this sentiment in his sixteenth letter by referring to the poor in spirit as those who follow the path of nothingness: "[T]he poor in spirit are happier and more constant in the midst of want because they have placed their all in nothingness, and in all things they thus find freedom of heart. O happy nothingness, and happy hiding place of the heart!"[39] For John happiness is found in nothingness.

Lastly, we turn to Meister Eckhart. Most of his surviving works are sermons. So, we can be assured that his mystical teaching was meant for everybody! Sermon 83 is a good starting point. This sermon includes a discussion on naming God and realizing all names are inadequate for God. In fact, our names for God say more about us than God. So, Eckhart urges his audience to sink into God: "You should wholly sink away from your youness, and dissolve into His Hisness, and your 'yours' and His 'His' should become so completely one 'Mine,' that with Him you understand His uncreated self-identity and His nameless Nothingness."[40] In essence, descend into God's self-identity and nameless nothingness; allow silence within, let go, and wait for the realization that your deepest self is the divine nothing. Our identity and the divine identity are one, which he expresses with the phrase: "your 'yours' and His 'His' should become so completely one 'Mine.'" This is a continuous state that is not

---

[39] *Ibid.*, 751
[40] *The Complete Mystical Works of Meister Eckhart*, 463

a new experience but a new way of experiencing, though beyond all experience! The journey for Eckhart is a stripping away of all the differences between us and God. We must become indistinguishable from God and only nothingness is indistinguishable, so we become nothing to become divine.

At the end of sermon 83, Eckhart exhorts us to love God: "You should love him as he is a non-God, a non-spirit, a non-person, a non-image, but as he is a pure, unmixed bright 'One,' separated from all duality; and in that One we should eternally sink down, out of something into nothing."[41] To love God we have to be stripped of all mediums, images, and thought. We cannot love God as any particular thing whether god, image, spirit, person or even as Ultimate Being. We must cease loving God as an object separate from us; rather we must love the One, the non-God, non-person, non-image, the nothing with whom we are one. We must love our deepest and truest Self, cut off from all duality. Realize divine oneness by "sinking down out of something into nothing." As indistinctly one with God we sink down out of the something-ness of our existence into the nothingness of God. Consent to the divine nothing annihilating us so we may live the great truth: I am the nothing.

In sermon 6, Eckhart has this wonderful line: "Those who are equal to nothing, they alone are equal to God. The divine reality is equal to nothing, and in it there is neither image nor form." When we are equal to nothing we are the same as God. Those who are nothing are God, for God is nothing. Since the divine reality is nothing, the divine is beyond image and form. Being equal to, or the same as, nothing requires the transcendence of all images (image itself) and all forms (even form itself). So, let God lead you

---

[41] *Meister Eckhart: The Essential Sermons, Commentaries, Treatises, and Defense*, trans. Edmund Colledge, NY: Paulist Press, 1981, 208.

beyond all mental images, even the ability to self-image, as well as all mental forms: the very form and structure of your consciousness. You then subtly awaken to who you really are: transcendent divinity.

Two more quotes are in order, for they are classic Eckhart. Both come from his famous sermon 52 on Matthew 5:3: "Blessed are the poor in spirit." Thus, the subject of the sermon is spiritual poverty. For Eckhart, spiritual poverty does not mean just physical poverty or dependence on God. He defines poverty of spirit in the following way: "A poor person wants nothing, knows nothing, and has nothing."[42] This formula says, as all our apophatic mystics have been saying, the way to the divine nothing is the way of nothingness. We must submit to God's annihilation of self. Nothingness is what true poverty is. It is interior poverty, which is ultimately about being poor in self-consciousness, poor in faculties that bolster the separate-self-sense: our willing must be left empty, our understanding must remain in unknowing, our very distinction from God must vanish.

Further on in sermon 52, Eckhart offers an unusual prayer: "I pray to God to free me of God."[43] With this prayer, Eckhart leads us into a deeper awareness of who we are. He is opening us up to mystical annihilation, for to become free of God is an annihilation of our separate self. So long as the ego is still our center we are unaware of our divine self. The point is to let go of all distinction between God and creatures and allow it to be nullified in nothing. Our prayer should be: "God, free me of the God who is, the God distinct from me who is an object separate from me. Rid me of divine being and help me realize I am You, divine nothing, in my deepest and eternal reality."

---

[42] *Ibid.*, 199
[43] *Ibid.*, 202

This brief examination of three apophatic mystics, the author of *The Cloud of Unknowing*, John of the Cross, and Meister Eckhart suffices to show that mystical nothingness is thoroughly rooted in Christian tradition. It is a clear path, a way of living in the Spirit of God. But, let us explore one final element in a spirituality of nothingness that comes out in Francis of Assisi and Therese of Lisieux. It is littleness or minority. Francis puts it this way in Admonition 19:

> Blessed is the servant who does not consider himself any better when he is praised and exalted by people than when he is considered worthless, simple, and looked down upon, for what a person is before God, that he is and no more.[44]

You are blessed and happy when other people's approval or disapproval means nothing to you. You are content to be nobody. Therese offers a similar perspective:

> We must consent to remain always poor and without strength, and this is the difficulty, for 'the truly poor in spirit, where do we find him? You must look for him from afar,' said the psalmist. He does not say that you must look for him among great souls, but 'from afar,' that is to say in lowliness, nothingness...let us love our littleness, let us love to feel nothing.[45]

---

[44] Francis of Assisi, *Francis of Assisi: The Saint*, NY: New City Press, 1999, 135.
[45] *Letters of St. Therese of Lisieux Volume II*, trans. John Clark, Washington, DC: ICS Publications, 1988, 999.

Nothingness is also lowliness, minority. It is being small, nobody, no one in particular, and no one special. It is the state of humility, just being what we are: nothing.

Now, this spirituality of nothingness places us in a radical state that is no state, no-mind, and unknowing. There is nothing to do to get God. There is nothing we need to know or can know of God. There is nothing distinguishing us from God. Meister Eckhart describes this well when he says the truly poor in spirit are those who "will nothing, know nothing, and have nothing." "Willing nothing" means we cannot control The divine or force spiritual growth. "Knowing nothing" is unknowing. We cannot comprehend the incomprehensible. "Having nothing" describes the spiritual attitude of non-possession: do not hold onto anything, including our independence and separation from God. In other words, Eckhart is talking about contemplation. Our "experience" of this self-emptying is a sharing in the self-emptying of the triune God. Our self-annihilation is a revelation of the nothingness of God.

We can also describe this process as "mystical crucifixion." We die with Christ on the cross when we are emptied out, with faith in nothing but God and attached to nothing at all. The human person vanishes into the Mystery of God's nothingness while hanging on the cross with Jesus. Crucified with Christ I vanish into the void of godless nothing. Joining Eckhart's prayer, "I pray God to free me of God," we let the God the Supreme Being vanish. We consent to God's deconstruction of our world, our ego, and our separate-self. Let all separation be negated. We allow our very selves to be annihilated into the void of godless nothing. This is the essence of contemplation. Thus, from our exploration of Christian apophatic mysticism we can see that the term "nothingness" has been a transcendent way to signify a dynamic state of prayer consciousness, the activity of God, and the very reality of God who is our deepest self.

# Chapter 3

# Nothingness in the Practice of Centering Prayer

A typical period of centering prayer may look something like this: you sit down, settle into your chair, and begin by gently saying your word. A few moments of peace may follow. Then, thoughts flood your mind. Or, maybe, thoughts crowd into your consciousness right away. You return ever-so-gently to your sacred word. Then again, there may be times when returning to the word is not so easy or so gentle. In fact, your thoughts and feelings may pummel you for some time. It can feel like we are always battling our thoughts. They just keep coming! And, often, they stick around. There might be times when a particular thought is very sticky and you then try hard to get rid of it. Then, you return ever-so-gently to your sacred word. Then, the thought comes back. Then, you return to your word. And, once again, the thought reappears! This cycle can continue the whole time of meditation. Or, once you introduce your word at the beginning, the next twenty minutes are spent thinking and you only realize that has been the case when your timer goes off. Of course, there may be other times when thoughts come and go freely while you are neither attracted to them nor repulsed by them. There's just refreshing silence. In fact, you may not even need your symbol at times, and all of a sudden your prayer time is over. You may reflect that your twenty to thirty minutes felt like two minutes.

All of the above scenarios and others are possible experiences of centering prayer. I want to share with you some insights about dealing with all of them in a more contemplative manner than *returning ever-so-gently to your sacred symbol* and complementary to *letting thoughts be just as they are*. I want to share with you how nothingness teaches us to handle our thoughts. Then, we will examine the relationship between nothingness and consent, the heart and soul of centering prayer.

To help our discussion, let us take a brief excursion into the different types of thoughts, and then answer the question, what is the problem with thinking? In *Open Mind, Open Heart* Thomas Keating considers five different kinds of thoughts: the ordinary wanderings of the imagination, interesting thoughts - either attractive or repulsive, insights of a theological or psychological nature, self-reflection, and primitive thoughts from the unloading of the unconscious.[46]

A quite ordinary part of centering prayer is our imagination running all over the place. Our minds tend to jump from one topic to the next through connections that are sometimes logical and sometimes not so logical. This is the monkey mind, and we can experience this in varying degrees. At times it feels like our minds are eternally restless. Other times, though, the imagination can feel quiet or maybe even lifeless. Nevertheless, it is usually like background music in a supermarket. We can easily let it be and even forget about it, but then there are times when we notice it, and still other times when it feels oppressive in our minds. As Keating says regarding these thoughts:

> Such thoughts are like the noise in the street floating through the window of an apartment where two people are carrying on a conversation. Their attention is firmly directed to each other, but they cannot avoid hearing the street noise. Sometimes they reach a point where they don't notice it at all.[47]

---

[46] Keating, *Open Mind, Open Heart*, 122-126
[47] *Ibid.*, 123

But, there are stickier thoughts - thoughts that tend to hang around and even plague us. These are thoughts with an emotional attraction. Such thoughts have an emotional tinge to them so that we either want to think about them or resist them entering our minds. There are thoughts we often desire to think about: thoughts that entertain, comfort, and delight us. And then, there are certain thoughts we would rather never enter our minds, thank you very much! These can be painful memories, confusing or negative thoughts, or any thought or perception that feels bad. We just want them out or never to come in. So, we naturally want to resist them.

More subtly, we can experience insightful thoughts. We can suddenly have a breakthrough psychological or spiritual idea. We will want to remember it, write it down, or develop it. The idea seems that important in the moment. But, it is just a defense mechanism of the ego, tasty bait to lure us out of interior silence. Submitting to such a deliberate thought will most definitely draw you out of contemplative silence. "Any deliberate thought brings you out."[48]

More subtly still, we can experience the last vestige of the ego: self-reflection. These are thoughts like, "I am really enjoying this." Or, "This is boring." Maybe even, "I'm finally experiencing no thoughts!" We innately want to posses the experience of interior silence, freedom, and joy. And we do that so we can remember how we got there, and what we have to do to reproduce the experience. We get possessive very quickly. Keating describes this type of thought as "one of the hardest things to handle in centering prayer."[49] We will discuss this type of thought more fully in the next chapter.

---

[48] *Ibid.*, 124
[49] *Ibid.*, 124-125

Keating describes the final type of thought as primitive emotions coming from the unloading of the unconscious.[50] Once we begin engaging a practice of interior silence, we remove the cover over our psychological unconscious. So, all the feelings we have repressed over a lifetime come out, often with great force. Additionally, I believe that a period of centering prayer that is very heavy with thoughts can function in the same manner: as an unloading of psychologically unconscious material. So, there can be times when we experience primitive emotions and other times when we experience a heavy barrage of thoughts. Both can be manifestations of the unloading of the unconscious emotions. These repressed feelings are typically some of the biggest obstacles to our innate oneness with God.

A more fundamental issue than the types of thoughts we experience in centering prayer, however, is the problem with thinking. So, what is the problem? Thinking reinforces the illusion of separation from God and all of creation. Eckhart Tolle has an apropos comment:

> About 80 to 90 percent of most people's thinking is not only repetitive and useless, but because of its dysfunctional and often negative nature, much of it is also harmful…This kind of compulsive thinking is actually an addiction…you derive your sense of self from the content and activity of your mind…As you grow up, you form a mental image of who you are, based on your personal and cultural conditioning. We may call this phantom self the ego. It consists of mind activity and can only be kept going through constant thinking.[51]

---

[50] *Ibid.*, 126
[51] Tolle, Eckhart, *The Power of Now*, Vancouver, B.C. and Novato, CA: Namaste and New World Publishing, 1999, 22.

Our addiction to thinking undergirds all other major addictions, whether to drugs or to more subtle addictions like control and approval.

We're addicted to thinking! Thinking is the primary attachment. Thinking reinforces our perceived alienation from God. We maintain separation from God by thinking. This, of course, is just as central for Keating: "The chief thing that separates us from God is the thought that we are separated from God. If we get rid of that thought, our troubles will be greatly reduced."[52] Many of us never realize that we are trapped by our minds. We judge, analyze, critique, discuss, and view everything in reality from the perspective of our addictive thinking. Therefore, we cannot see what is right in front of us: the mystery of the presence of God totally available and for the taking here and now. More to the point, we presume we can grasp everything with our thinking, with our minds. Our addictive thinking shrinks reality down to our size. All of this keeps us separate from God, other people, and indeed all of reality.

The apophatic mystics would say, "Well of course!" They remind us, first of all, that the nothingness of God cannot be grasped by thinking. The divine mystery transcends the mind. Our thoughts of God are just that, thoughts. They are not God. Thus, our practice of centering prayer must transcend thinking. This much we know, however. Centering prayer involves letting go of all thoughts, all thinking. "The method of centering prayer is designed to turn off the ordinary flow of thoughts that reinforces our habitual way of thinking of ourselves and of looking at the world."[53] In this way, interior silence takes root in us.

---

[52] Keating, *Open Mind, Open Heart*, 33
[53] *Ibid.*, 120

Keating has taught that the way to handle thoughts is to ignore them, let them be. Accept them as they are and go beyond them without effort. Just let them go. "Resist no thought, retain no thought, react emotionally to no thought."[54] Just rest in God and rest from thinking. However, Keating has also described centering prayer in the following way:

> Doing this prayer is not *doing* nothing, but *being* nothing...Jesus' invitation is to become 'no thing,' i.e., not attached or over-identified with anything. God is not a thing, but all things. We must become detached even from our ideas of God.[55]

So, our contemplative practice is not even limited by the contemplative attitude of *just being*. Centering prayer journeys into the vast unknown of mystical nothingness.

So, let's go deeper into our centering prayer practice with nothingness. According to the teachings of the apophatic mystics, what do we do with our thinking? Nothing! Do not do anything at all with your thoughts. Instead, let all your thoughts, let all thinking, fade away into nothing. Do not engage them, resist them, retain them, or react to them. When you think your thoughts, just nothing. Allow non-thinking nothingness. Do not try to meditate. This is one of Frenette's most helpful comments. He says, "rest in God without trying to find God, without even trying to meditate."[56] This is a good initial description of practicing with nothingness. Do not try *to do* anything at all. Do not try *to be* anything at all. Do not even *be*.

---

[54] *Ibid.*, 127
[55] "Centering Prayer and Resting in God," Contemplative Outreach News Vol.29, #1 December 2012.
[56] Frenette, 19

Of course, even when we allow non-thinking nothingness, we will find that our minds still go on and on. We cannot stop the movement of thought in prayer. We can be filled with thoughts - even the effortful striving for rest and nothing, even thoughts of rest and nothing. Yet, we're already in God! Rest from striving, rest from a goal, rest from trying to change your mind with its endless thoughts, and fabricated experiences. What are you striving for? Is there too much striving and effort in your prayer practice? That is an obstacle to nothingness. Let go of trying to get somewhere in prayer. Effort only bolsters the ego. And our effort can manifest as trying to do the practice right. Frenette says a big initial obstacle in centering prayer is rigidity.[57] This is our self-conscious effort to do the method right, trying too hard to do a technique for an observable result. Prayer is not a technique. Remember, we are loving God, and love is for nothing. Therefore, we are not aiming at some observable result. We are not aiming for any result at all.

Our effort can also manifest as resistance to some thoughts we would rather not flow through us. Resisting thoughts only creates more ego. Opposing your thoughts merely reinforces the ego and the separate self-sense. So, we may be experiencing unwanted thoughts as well as our effort to resist them. In this case all we can do is *nothing*: accept your experience of prayer as it is without attaching to it. Just accept and ignore it. When you reach the edge of your limits, stay open in dark faith without expecting God to do something in particular or even at all.

Often, contemplative teaching will advise us to handle thoughts by *just being*. Be. Return to the word. However, these are commands. They are things for *you* to do. Rather, the teaching here is: *nothing*. Just nothing. No command, because there is nothing for *you* to do - in fact

---

[57] *Ibid.*, 24

there is nothing of *you* at all. This is ab
transparency in prayer. We could also say just si
stillness. But these can easily be felt as or in
merely isolated experiences. Just nothing is dee
experience. Remember, we cannot, in actuality
nothing.

Nothingness: you do not even have to
silence there is nothing for you to be, nothing fo
nothing of you at all. This is non-meditation;
meditate. Just nothing. *To be* still has a shad
doing and effort. Nothingness is absolute effor
mind and no self - only the mystery of God wh
"Just being" still implies a substance relating to a substance, which is far too dualistic for the divine mystery. In the nothingness we do not even try to let go of thoughts. Simply drop all thinking and allow thoughts to pass by with no effort to remove them. The point of centering prayer is not to hang onto a symbol, but to let go into the mystery of God. With nothingness, not only is there no symbol, there is no return to a symbol - there is no return at all.

To be clear, handle thoughts during centering prayer with *nothing*. No resisting thoughts, no retaining thoughts, no reacting to thoughts, no returning to a symbol. Just nothing within. If you start thinking, you can still let thoughts go promptly by returning to your word. More deeply, you can let thoughts go promptly by letting them be. Still deeper, just nothing. Nothingness is the vanishing of thinking - even if there are still thoughts! As Keating reminds us, "to have thoughts is not the problem. Thinking *about* thoughts is the problem."[58] Let your thoughts vanish into the nothing. To be clear, the word is still available if needed. Nothingness in centering prayer means the letting go of the gentle return as well as all thinking. Both nothingness

---

[58] Keating, *Open Mind, Open Heart*, 39

in centering prayer and the ever-so-gentle return, however, can be present in a single session of centering prayer.

Savor the following "instructions" for entering into the nothingness: Allow thoughts to disappear; allow them to fade away into nothingness. Let all you are and all you are doing be nothing. Let thoughts, experience, and self-reflection fade into oblivion. Just nothing: totally open and nondual receptivity. Let your mind be blank. Vanish into nothing; sheer nothing; just nothing; effortless nothing; let nothing; non-thinking nothing. Allow all your thinking to dissolve into nothing, and remain there in the nothing. Drop all thinking and let nothingness: Let nothingness surface; let the nothingness arise from deep within you; Let the nothingness awaken within you and as you.

Beneath thoughts, experiences, and even being itself: nothing. This is, simply, very simply, nothing. In centering prayer: just effortless and open nothing. We let nothingness in. We allow nothingness to replace our efforts and thoughts and feelings. Allow nothingness to rise up within and reign interiorly. For nothingness to reign within, our active thinking must halt. And that is what it is like to practice contemplative nothingness. It is the cessation of all mental activity. No matter what is going in your head, you just drop it - all of it. This simple end to thinking is the voiding and vanishing of all interior self-talk. The cessation of all mental activity necessarily includes an unhooking of attachment to thinking, of interest in or aversion to the contents of the mind, and an immediate reduction to nothingness.

Alertness and awake-ness characterize our disposition in the nothingness. Often, our experience of centering prayer can seem dreamy - as in our attention floats in and out of thinking as if we were dreaming at times. Our intention and general awareness can become lost in thinking in a very subtle way. It is easy to drift away in thoughts and start to fantasize about some delight, think about a plan, or mull over an issue we are having. These are all occasions to allow nothingness and not let oneself drift off into thinking. Let the nothingness wake you up. Allow alert nothingness. Remain in the nothingness and remain vigilant.

Alertness, though, does not equal concentration. Centering prayer does not work with concentration. Rather, intention and general awareness characterize centering prayer. Concentration and focused attention often describe eastern practices. People can confuse and conflate eastern meditation practices with centering prayer, but they are distinct. The difference between Eastern (Hindu and Buddhist) meditation and centering prayer, as well as the "non-meditation" or "meta-meditation" I am describing is that eastern meditation exercises concentration and one-pointed-ness of mind. Applied to centering prayer (or any contemplative practice from the East or the West), nothingness emphasizes no-pointed-ness of mind.

Thoughts will always pass. They always do. All perceptions go away if we wait long enough. We are letting all thinking pass. So, let thoughts release themselves.[59] Everything passes. But, we are also yielding to the disappearance of the "structure" of the prayer: our ever-so-gentle return to the word. We even allow a subtle return to silence to fade away. Let the form of your method, however subtle, release itself.[60] Even a subtle return is still an action of ours. And, the nothingness is all about the loss of self. Of course, if we need it, returning to the word is still okay. If needed, ever-so-gently return to your sacred symbol. Otherwise, rest from returning,[61] and effortless nothing.

---

[59] A phrase I received on a retreat with David Frenette, "Deeper Center, Living Prayer," March 2010, see Frenette, ch.13
[60] Another phrase I received from Frenette, see Frenette, ch.6
[61] see Frenette, ch.3

Regarding the return to the word, the sacred word is not a way into silence. Silence is already there and we naturally want to go there. The sacred word allows us space to do so. It helps us consent to God, allowing us to go where we naturally want to go, but had obstacles in our way. And we naturally want the divine silence. Keating advises us:

> When you become aware that you are thinking about or engaged with some thought, return to the sacred word as the expression of your intent. The effectiveness of this prayer does not depend on how distinctly you say the sacred word or how often, but rather on the gentleness with which you introduce it in the beginning and the promptness with which you return to it when you are engaged mentally or emotionally with some thought.[62]

The word facilitates the letting go of thoughts. It is not a technique aiming at a result: as in, return to the word and experience silence. Remember, have no expectations. The sacred word, then, should not be used as an object to get you into silence. This is dualistic. If needed, ever-so-gently return to your word and effortlessly enjoy silence - whether you experience it or not! For, to experience some*thing* is also dualistic. Just silence, effortless nothingness.

So, this contemplative nothingness means thoughtless, effortless, experience-less silence. Thoughts float by and you have no interest in them. Our minds can be quiet on a deep level yet have thoughts and feelings. There is no concern about them or attachment to them. "By interior silence we refer primarily to a state in which we do not become attached to the thoughts as they go by."[63] Just nothing in whatever is

---

[62] Keating, *Open Mind, Open Heart*, 121-122
[63] *Ibid.*, 43

going on - empty of form, empty of effort, empty of struggle, motionless within and without. Do not resist; do not fight. Just allow your consciousness to be drained of content, its structure, and being itself. Such sheer receptivity deepens into the divine receptivity. This is prayer in secret, which means a lack of content, activity, and self. There is nothing to do and nothing to be. In the nothingness, the Spirit draws us into utterly naked and nondual faith.

In the nothing, psychological experience is irrelevant because the nothingness is deeper than experience. Further, as I just stated, experience is inherently dualistic: there's the experiencer and the experienced, which is mediated by feelings, thoughts, interpretations. The nothingness is there without our experiencing it. Thus it requires the purest and most naked faith. Yet detachment from thoughts is still important. We let all thinking vanish into nothing, even feeling the nothingness or feeling rest or peace or interior silence. Just pure nothingness, which we can't feel or experience. In the nothingness there is no sustained perceiver, no inner witness. The nothingness is deeper. In fact, there is no perceiver, no perceiving, and no perceived - no perception at all. Nothingness means no attention to anything at all, let alone concentration. Transcend perception and experience.

Gradually we awaken to a wonderful truth: the inner nothingness of contemplative prayer is the divine reality. But, we still don't focus on any *experience* of nothingness. This inner nothingness transcends or is deeper than experience. For, in the nothingness we even lose the sense that God is: we realize non-thinking godless nothing. Just nothing is a most receptive and nondual contemplative practice. Perhaps we could call it a non-practice or a meta-practice? For, *you* are not *doing* at all; *you* are not *being* at all; there's nothing from *you*. It's only God. We could even call it non-meditation.

So, do not make the nothingness happen; do not force it as an experience. If you find you are trying too hard, resisting thoughts, focusing on feeling something, or even settling into an experience of nothingness, it is usually ego. As Tolle says, "Your mind is trying to make nothing into something. The moment you make it into something, you have missed it. Nothing…cannot become an object of knowledge."[64] Instead, sink into simple, non-experiential, and purely divine nothingness.

Practicing with nothingness follows Jesus' command to deny self and to lose the self. "A very intimate kind of self-denial is necessary in this prayer...It involves the denial of what we are most attached to, namely, our own inmost thoughts and feelings and the source from which they come, the false self."[65] We are surrendering our very selves unconditionally in the nothingness. It is pure loss of the self.

I invite us to permit nothingness to arise within. Once we consent, we see that, without effort, we disidentify with our thoughts and our feelings - especially our thinking. So, nothingness is an invitation to let self go, to let self vanish and disappear into God. The nothingness, however, is not a *self-induced* void of mental activity. It is, however, void of all thinking, feeling, and experience. But, faith, hope, and love are still active. This is so because of our intention: to love God, or, more simply, God is your intention - just God.

As centering prayer matures nothingness becomes our intention; nothingness assumes our consent. Recall that intention and consent are the heart and soul of centering prayer. Keating says, "Centering prayer is more intention than attention. There is no way of knowing God directly in this life except by means of pure faith, which is darkness to

---

[64] Tolle, 137
[65] Keating, *Open Mind, Open Heart*, 124

all the faculties."[66] As we yield to the nothing, we feel less and less need to re-affirm our consent with the sacred symbol or even with a formal prayer of words or thoughts to begin and end the prayer period. We just enjoy silence and love God. Keating points to the deep identity of silence and the sacred word: "Interior silence *is* the sacred word at its deepest level."[67] This means that interior silence *is* consent. Our simple presence is our deep "yes" to God.

There is a potential issue with our intention, though. We can objectify God through our intention. We can treat God as a goal for us to get. We may use our intention as a means to an end. God, though, is not an object outside us to be experienced on our terms. Our thinking will always attempt to grasp God and so bring God down to our level. Our ego will always want to meet God on its terms. When we treat God as an object, even through our intention, we can make God into some*thing* to experience on our terms.

Whereas if our intention is just God - read here, just nothing - we can shed this objectifying attitude and let God really be God: mystery beyond mystery beyond all the limitations of our language, of our thinking, of our experience, and even of being. Nothingness is consent - but not consent *to* God. This still implies separation. Nothingness is nondual. Nothingness is nondual consent, Trinitarian consent. Through the nothing, your consent becomes divine consent. For in us, through us, and as us God consents as God: Father pouring out the divine self into the Son, Son emptying back into the Father - all through the Holy Spirit. The Holy Trinity is self-emptying, self-annihilating, and loving consent. Indeed, according to Keating, "To consent to God's presence is His presence."[68]

---

[66] *Ibid.*, 42
[67] *Ibid.*, 40
[68] *Ibid.*, 36

Our consent becomes nondual, indistinct from the divine nothing. Then, the nothingness of our centering prayer, the nothingness of contemplation, the nothingness that we are is this very same divine nothingness eternally loving in a self-annihilating manner as Trinity.

Experientially, as you love God, it may seem like God is not even there. But, on the contrary, in the nothingness God's love becomes utterly real. For, as you allow nothingness you enter into self-annihilation - you continue kenosis, the self-emptying of Christ in the Paschal Mystery. Non-thinking godless nothing annihilates you - for God is empowering you to leave your thinking, even the ever-present thought of self. God, in other words, is reducing you to nothing in nothing. Centering prayer, then, is an exercise in nonresistant, open, and annihilated presence: mystical absence, un-thinking nothingness. Commenting on the prayer of Jesus, Nemeck and Coombs note a connection:

> 'He emptied himself' (Ph.2:7). In the context of the prayer of Jesus, 'kenosis' means that he opened and surrendered himself in order that his divinity could more and more permeate his humanity...God has actually communicated himself through only one way: Jesus Christ, by way of kenosis (Ph.2:7). Consequently, there is only one 'way' that we can commune with him—the same 'way': by being emptied.[69]

Allowing non-thinking nothingness is to be one with the self-emptying of Christ Crucified. Practicing nothingness in centering prayer is a way to follow and identify with Christ Crucified. In the same way, it is also a pure act of love for God, just as Jesus' sacrifice on the cross was.

---

[69] Nemeck, 34

# Chapter 4

## Self-Reflection: The Objectifying Thought

The greatest obstacle along the spiritual journey is the illusion of separation: that we are cut off from God, others, and all of creation. This chapter will describe this illusion and one major way our egos maintain this illusion: objectification. Often, our egos deploy this strategy during centering prayer. At other times, it reveals itself in the course of our relationships. No matter what, though, objectification blocks the nothingness. It keeps the divine at bay. It constitutes the walls of the ego's fortress defending against reality. The great call of the spiritual life is to be humble. And being humble means to see reality as it is. So, in this chapter we will examine, first, duality, the root of separation, then the ego's main attachment (the mind), culminating in the objectifying thought of self-reflection. Afterwards, we will take a look at the antidote to this great illusion: self-forgetfulness and the nondual nothingness.

The great illusion has been called duality. It means "two-ness." There is a subject and an object. I, the perceiver, am the subject while all of reality is an object to me. I am distanced from reality. I am observing it but not a part of it. In other words, the illusion is that God and I are two and not one. So, the problem is we think we are cut off from God and we grow up with this frame of reference. At the center of this frame of reference is the self. We see reality through our homemade self: our egos. Simon Tugwell, a contemporary Dominican friar, says:

> It is precisely our "existence" as independent subjects that is our original fall. It is our standing -

out (ex-sistentia) from the primordial wholeness and oneness of all things in God which breaks our union with him. As long as there is an "I" which confronts God, there is no real union with him.[70]

God, as we have been saying, is not an object for us to experience on our own terms, that is, on the terms of the ego. To be a self is to be self-conscious and this means we are on one side of duality: we are the subject to God who is our object. This consciousness totally contradicts our innate oneness with God and all reality. For, to be one with God is also to be one with the entire cosmos: from the tiniest quark to the biggest galaxy. Tugwell, again:

> It is good that we exist; our existence is part of the richness of the world of God's making. But our consciousness should be so totally united with God that there is no room left for any separate consciousness of ourselves.[71]

So, we feel separated from God. This feeling of separation is our ordinary psychological experience of the human condition. It is the cause of our efforts to look for happiness down every path that we can possibly envision when actually it is right under our noses. When we perceive ourselves as separate we live in fear, because life seems uncertain and dangerous. Conflict within and without becomes the norm. What maintains this sense of separation is our minds, or, rather, being identified with our thinking and our feelings.

---

[70] Tugwell, Simon, "Preface" to *The Cloud of Unknowing*, Classics of Western Spirituality, NY: Paulist Press, 1981, xxi
[71] Tugwell, xxii

Dualism functions by turning everything into an object. First and foremost, we turn ourselves into objects even while remaining subjects. The split between subject and object reflects a fundamental objectification. As a culture we are all too familiar with this phenomenon. We will twist any created reality into an object, a thing, which will inevitably have the characteristics of an idol. That is, we turn created realities into things we use. We manipulate them to our own devices and for our own ends. As Keating would say, we attempt to squeeze all the security, affection, and control we can get out of these objects. We make people into objects when we use exploit them for economic gain or for sexual pleasure, for instance. To treat any creature as a thing is to engage in an addiction. It is to form an attachment to the thing because we are using it to get ultimate happiness. In the end, this objectification will make us miserable as it leads us away from true happiness and ultimate salvation: God.

Now, objectification roots itself in our spirits through a foundational dualism: splitting subject and object, splitting reality. As a result, all we experience is this separation we have been discussing. We do not perceive the underlying unity of all creation in the divine spirit. The major mental structure keeping separation alive is self-reflection. It is at the core of our attachment to thinking. It is the last bastion of the ego. It is a key feature of identifying our self with thinking. It is the mechanism of objectification. Further, the tendency to be possessiveness follows this thought. We will explore how self-reflection is a manifestation of subtle clinging.

As we saw earlier, self-reflection is one of the thoughts we will encounter in our practice of centering prayer. Keating describes the experience of this thought during centering prayer:

> [a] desire to reflect on what is happening may arise…You are being offered a choice between reflecting on what is going on and letting go of the experience. If you let go, you go into deeper interior silence. If you reflect, you come out and have to start over. There will be a lot of starting over.[72]

We maintain our separation by self-reflection. And reflecting on self tends towards possessiveness. It is not that it is greedy possessiveness. It is that when we are locked in self-reflection we tend to regard our world with possessiveness. In other words, self-reflection circles around the *self*. The reference point is the self. Thus, we cannot help but relate to everything from the self-perspective. And that tends to make us possessive.

Furthermore, by reflecting during our prayer we reduce God to an experience we want to possess and understand. And, we can neither possess nor understand God. Keating describes self-reflection as "taking a photograph" of our experience:

> Every reflection is like a photograph of reality. It isn't our original experience; it is a commentary on it. Just as a picture only approximates reality, so every reflection is one step back from experience as it actually is. When we experience the presence of God, if we can just not think about it, we can rest in it for a long time.[73]

And this photo of reality is some*thing* we can hold onto, some*thing* we can possess and return to when it suits us. We objectify. In this way, self-reflection keeps us separate from

---

[72] Keating, *Open Mind, Open Heart*, 124
[73] *Ibid.*, 83

reality. We relate to everything from the self as our central reference point.

Self-reflection means we relentlessly think of ourselves; self is our first and central thought. This suffocating narcissism can be overcome only through grace, specifically the grace of self-forgetfulness. To forget self is to realize the nothingness of God. Keating reminds us,

> So long as you feet united with God, it cannot be full union. So long as there is a thought, it is not full union. The moment of full union has no thought. You don't know about it until you emerge from it. In the beginning it is so tenuous that you may think you were asleep.[74]

Feeling God is still a thought. We are still in the subject-object mode. We are still in dualism. The point is to let self-reflection go. But, once we try to do this we turn it into a project for the ego to accomplish. Self is back in charge. Rather, we have to allow God to dissolve self-reflection in the divine nothingness, even though self-reflection is not bad. It is a stage on the journey:

> You have to go through greater self-awareness in order to let God awaken you to pure awareness ...The Spirit enfolds your self-consciousness; your self-awareness, as your will, your effort, releases on its own.[75]

Contemplation, then, accepts God on God's terms, but without possessiveness. "Trying to hang on to God's

---

[74] *Ibid.*, 69
[75] Frenette, 54

presence is like trying to hang on to the air."[76] Accepting God on God's terms means to accept nothingness. It means we let all thoughts go. We let all thoughts dissolve into nothingness. Now, while we are resting in the nothing, God is waking us up to the divine life, light, and love already present within us. This awakening happens beyond self-reflection and self.

> Letting go and not reflecting on what you are doing is the correct way to conduct yourself in this prayer. The method doesn't consist in how you sit or in the length of time you give, but in how you handle the thoughts that arise.[77]

We handle self-reflection by letting it vanish into nothing, without seeing it as a problem. Let self-reflection release itself. Let God free you of the reflective-self. Even noticing when you are engaged with your thoughts is itself a thought. Let this fade into nothing as well. Even when you are aware of no thoughts, that is still a thought, a self-reflective thought.

> If you are aware of no thoughts, you are aware of something and that is a thought. If at that point you can lose the awareness that you are aware of no thoughts, you will move into *pure consciousness*. In that state there is no consciousness of self.[78]

Let this thought vanish into nothing. We cannot actively lose self-consciousness but we can permit it to happen. We can hand it over to God. We can let all self-focus and self-talk

---

[76] Keating, *Open Mind Open Heart*, 89
[77] *Ibid.*, 87
[78] *Ibid.*, 68-69

dissolve in the mystery of the God beyond God who takes us ever-beyond.

Let all experiences of God vanish into nothing. Let even the experience of rest release itself. Lose the awareness that you are aware. Let self-reflection dissolve. Savor these phrases: *Non-reflective nothing; Selfless nothing.* Let thoughts, experience, self-reflection fade into oblivion. Let the subtle thought of having no thoughts release itself. Allow the thought, feeling, and experience of nothingness to disappear in the nothingness.

In contemplation we refuse to talk to ourselves. The internal dialogue keeps us focused on ourselves, for it is self-validating, self-affirming, and self-referential. We rehearse and replay our story, thus solidifying our opinions and judgments. But, contemplation takes the focus off of self. In fact, in contemplation our focus dissolves into the nothingness. The core of contemplation is a state of nothing-mind, in which you are alert and detached but not thinking.

Nothing-mind is this: The one who is aware disappears along with whatever was the object of consciousness. This is what divine oneness is. There is no reflection of self. Divine oneness is devoid of thinking. If you are actually not thinking, there is not even the thought that you are not thinking.[79] In this vein, Keating quotes St. Antony of Egypt as saying, "Perfect prayer is not to know that you are praying."[80] Prayer without knowing it's prayer is non-reflective and secret, it's just God: non-reflective silence and non-awareness. Non-reflection is unknowing is secrecy. The unknowing and secrecy of contemplation is selflessness or self-forgetfulness. Frenette says, "in pure contemplation, you also allow the awareness of God to fall away."[81]

---

[79] *Ibid.*, 69
80 *Ibid.*, 92
81 Frenette, 98

Because there is no subject, there is no object. There is nothing. This is nonduality. We allow even the awareness of nothingness to vanish into nothing.

Let us return to Meister Eckhart to unpack this. Eckhart refers to the deepest dimension of the human as intellect. And, for Eckhart, the intellect is nothing. According to Eckhart, there is an untouched point in the human person that connects immediately with God. This is the intellect. Since the intellect is nothing we are indistinguishable from the divine because the divine is nothing. Hence, insofar as I am intellect I am divine; I become the transcendent nothingness. But, for Eckhart we are always created finite beings distinct from God. He holds both together as paradox. Scholar Denys Turner says, "The intellect is not distinguishable in its character of being a 'nothing' from the divine nature which is 'nothing'."[82] Eckhart is able to say this because one of the ways he locates our identity with God is in the intellect. This is where we are uncreated. In his Parisian Questions, Eckhart says, "intellect, as such, is a nothing."[83]

Now for Eckhart, God as nothing transcends the "this and that" of creature: God is indistinct. Because God is indistinct and because God and creatures are distinct, what distinguishes God from creatures is the divine indistinction. So, if it is God's nature to be indistinct, "neither this nor that," then it follows that God's primary name is "intellect." And, as we saw, intellect is nothing. Thus, we are back to Eckhart's radical apophatic theology: God is nothing. Turner declares, "Here, then, Eckhart draws the startling conclusion...intellect is God."[84] Intellect is nothing. God is

---

82 Turner, Denys, *The Darkness of God: Negativity in Christian Mysticism*, Cambridge: Cambridge University Press, 1995, 152.
83 quoted in Turner, 158
84 *Ibid.*, 165

intellect. God is nothing. The highest and most transcendent dimension of the human person is intellect. The deepest reality of the human person is nothing. The human person's deepest self is God.

With the intellect, according to Eckhart, "the soul works in nonbeing and so follows God who works in nonbeing."[85] Turner then says, "In this respect the intellect is therefore indistinguishable from the divine...as intellect, no distinction can be made between it and God."[86] In other words, insofar as I am intellect I am the divine indistinction. "Hence I am, *qua* intellect, God."[87] But, again, this does not mean I am in no way distinct from God: "in so far as I am not intellect I am created."[88] God is nothing; God is intellect; intellect is nothing; and insofar as I am intellect I am the divine nothing. In my deepest reality I am nothing. God's nature is to be nothing distinct, nothing in particular, so nothing at all. So, insofar as I am a something for which God is, I am not the nothing which God is. Beyond all somethings, I identify with the divine nothing.

To realize identity with the nothing we must let the self go completely. As Keating says, "This prayer is an exercise in letting go of everything including your own self-identity."[89] This means we let go of a relating self, the self-in-relationship. The nothingness calls us to transcend our relationship with God. Go beyond *relating* to God and *relationship* with God to oneness and nonduality: nothing.

Thus, nothingness is no subject-object split, nonduality. The divine nothingness, in this sense, is not simply the opposite of being. Nothingness is not just privation, but

---

85 *Meister Eckhart: Teacher and Preacher*, 258
86 Turner, 158
87 *Ibid.*, 165
88 *Ibid.*
[89] Keating, *Open Mind, Open Heart*, 89

absolute transcendence of all that is and therefore one and the same with all that is. The nondual nothing reconciles the opposites of existence and non-existence because the nothing transcends the opposites of being and non-being. The nothing reconciles the paradox of being both distinct from God and yet one and the same as God. Realizing the nondual nothingness is a matter of self-annihilation. Tugwell suggests this:

> The abolition of any clear notion of God in contemplative unknowing thus goes with the abolition of any clear awareness of the knowing subject. One must approach God in such nakedness that it is clothed not even in itself. Only so can it allow the "nothing" in the "nowhere" of contemplation. Only "nobody" constitutes no obstacle to this work...If God is to be all in all, there is no room for us as a separate center or focus of existence...But this "self-naughting," though it means that we must lose our consciousness of ourselves, is actually the way that we *become* ourselves.[90]

The self is the great issue in the spiritual life. If we stop and reflect on what keeps us from seeing God in all things, from praying always, we find that it is the self. Because we constantly refer everything back to the self, because the self is the organizing principle of our consciousness, we will always experience contemplation in a dualistic manner. Contemplation will remain one experience among many experiences. However, in the process of healing and transformation through contemplation, God replaces the self as the organizing principle of our experience with the divine

---

[90] Tugwell, xxii.

presence. And then, in the process of mystical annihilation - when the divine nothing reduces the soul to nothing - God destroys the very structures of consciousness, the very duality inherent in the human mind, so that we pass from transformed self to selflessness: pure nothingness in which there is nothing but God who is nothing.

So, regarding our contemplative practice and our contemplative life, the point is to ignore yourself, to let the self go as soon as you see that you are becoming the center of your interest. Do so to bring all your attention, intention, and love to God. We forget self in God. The self dissolves in the divine nothing. Here is the point of becoming nothing: the self is the biggest "thing" in the way of realizing unity with God. So, when you think of self, allow nothingness.

# Chapter 5

# Nothingness in Daily Life

So far we have seen how the nothingness awakens during prayer. But the point of contemplation is not just to sit for the twenty to thirty minutes of intentional silence. Rather, the point is the contemplative state: realizing oneness with God in daily life. So, I offer you the practice of nothingness in daily life. Simply stated, in daily life, just nothing. But let us develop this a bit by looking at the practice, offering some comments on it, applying the practice to some real life scenarios, and connecting nothingness with social justice. Here is the practice:

<u>The Practice of Nothingness</u>:
Just nothing - in prayer and daily life
No attachment, no possessions, no ego;
No comfort zones, no private time, no comments
No fear, no exclusion, no shame;
No revenge, no brooding, no violence
No comparisons, no goals, no expectations;
No assumptions, no agenda, no excuses
No illusion, no addiction, no judgment;
No attention, no perception, no experience
No thinking, no feeling, no self-reflection;
No self, no other, no being,
Let all you are and all you are doing be reduced to nothing.
Simply nothing; Effortless nothing; Silent Nothing;
Open Nothing; Divine Nothing; Same Nothing;
Nothing, Nothing, Nothing

This formula has a few sections: the opening line "Just nothing - in prayer and daily life." Then, there are a number of "no" phrases. These phrases point out what we need to let go of, inner obstacles to the divine. Then, a summary statement: " Let all you are and all you are doing be reduced to nothing." Finally, the formula ends with some "nothing" terms: simply nothing, effortless nothing, etc.

In a dramatic fashion, the practice of nothingness shifts our attitudes and our priorities. The practice involves remaining in nothingness - that interior state of non-clinging and open fresh space - all day long. It is letting the self become nothing, forgetting oneself to center totally and exclusively on the mystery of God. All of the "no" phrases point to the obstacles that we need to let go of, to what takes a back seat to God in our everyday life. These phrases, however are not meant to communicate that these obstacles must be absolutely absent from our experience. Feelings and thought will be with us. Assumptions, expectations, perception, and experience walk with us. We cannot cease to exist. So, when I say "no self, no other, no being" I mean: do not let any of these realities occupy God's place. In short, have no idols. Let everything else become nothing. Let everything else recede into the background. Now, remember, we lose nothing good. When God is our center we cherish all more than we did before. So, we will love our families and friends even more. We will love them beyond addiction, shame, revenge, compassion, and without any self-centered agenda. Rooted in the mystery of mercy we will love divinely.

After the "no" phrases comes more nihilistic language: "let all you are and all you are doing be reduced to nothing." Let self die in daily life. Deny yourself and carry your cross on a daily basis. This line means forget yourself. It means, especially, let *all you are doing* fade away and dissolve. Let self and effort fizzle out. Positively, let your whole love, attention, and presence be wrapped up entirely in God. Seek nothing but God; enjoy nothing but God. Enjoy nothing but nothing.

The "nothing" terms conclude the formula. These terms give us the characteristics of living mystical nothingness. The nothingness is simple, not complicated. Effort has no place here. Noise and words and thoughts we leave behind. The nothingness keeps us open, not closed down. In fact, the nothingness is God, and it is us. And with these "nothing" lines, "simple nothing, divine nothing, same nothing," etc. I end the practice of nothingness. I offer it to you that you may enjoy your identity with God in the nothingness and mercy of divine mystery. We are one in the nothing. Enjoy it!

How does the practice of nothingness work, though? How do we do it? To put it plainly, we carry the state of interior nothingness from our time of centering prayer into our daily lives. When anything comes up that normally interferes with our relationships - as in an attachment or a pattern of behavior that damages us or others - we allow nothingness. Just nothing. We disidentify with whatever it is. More specifically, we disidentify with our *clinging* to whatever it is. Disidentify with all your feelings. Disidentifying with feelings is *just nothing*.

This practice requires no small amount of self-honesty. For, we must notice all the ego strategies going on within. Practicing nothingness demands a serious dedication to the truth about oneself. Nothingness can allow for illusions, no lies, no self-deception - much less deceiving others (whether consciously or unconsciously). In the nothingness we consent to having all our secrets purged, all our defenses torn down. Awareness is a necessity, that is, awareness of what our particular attachment is, of what we are feeling, of what is really going on.

But, keep in mind, that this awareness is not appropriate during centering prayer. We do not look at our thoughts or our attachments. We simply let them go. More to the point, the actual practice of nothingness takes us beyond awareness even while using it. So, even though I recommend being aware of your inner world, when I counsel practicing with nothingness I mean to say "go beyond awareness" by letting the mind rest in nothing.

With this understanding, we discover that we can disidentify with our feelings. How? By nothingness. When you have a negative feeling, or when you notice you are attached to something, or when you are acting out of the ego, effortlessly allow all you are thinking, all you are doing, and all you *are* to dissolve into nothing. The patterns and feelings may still be raging in you - for instance you may still feel anger or sadness - but in the nothingness we discover these feelings and patterns are not who we are. We discover they are all part of our ego. So, without much effort at all we can let these negative feelings and patterns pass through us and not act them out. In doing so, we realize that change is simple and then our whole world changes. For, we thought reality was identical with our inner egoic state. When we are in the nothingness, though, we see that only then does our inner state match up with reality. And herein we find out reality is absolutely delightful, because God is reality.

But, let us probe this a bit further. Practicing nothingness in daily life means holding tension. First, we hold emotional tension. Our feelings may be telling us one thing when reality is wholly on another page. The two just are not matching up. When we realize this, our emotions still may not be there. So, we have to suffer them. We let them be in us. We do not engage them just as we do not engage our thoughts during prayer. We allow our feelings to vanish into the nothingness even when it does not seem like they ever will. In this case, we keep remaining in the nothingness.

Talking with a therapist, spiritual director, friend, or spouse may be needed. But, we will still have to deal with these feelings on our own. Otherwise, we pass them on to the people around us.

Second, we hold the tension of paradoxes in our lives: how can we be sinful yet loved by God? Why do I still want to pray when I don't experience God at all? Why do I stay on the journey when I don't seem to be making any progress at all? Discovering our own self-deceptions can be a very painful experience: How can I have lied to myself yet still be a good person? How can anyone love me after what I have done? Amidst all these seeming contradictions, we remain nothing.

Beyond letting go of particular obstacles to love, the practice of nothingness means enjoying nothing but nothing - meaning nothing but God the nothing. In this dimension of practicing nothingness, do not look at anything. Do not look at yourself. This is to let go of ego, of all self. Forget self. In practice this means not being concerned with yourself and putting yourself aside. Whenever you find you are subjecting everything to yourself, allow nothingness. But, lest you think you then look at God, remember nothingness is nondual. So, do not even look at God. For, that would be to treat God as an object. This is to rejoice in God as God – not as the image you have of God. Let God be God: nothing. And let this be enough for you. Nothing else is needed. This is your happiness: nothingness.

Now, ignoring oneself has the implication that we also forget ourselves during times that have typically increased self-consciousness: times of despair, failure, weakness, sin, guilt and shame. Moreover, we can focus on self too much when we think too highly of ourselves, when we get what we want, or when we plan to get what we want. We can even transfer this self-focus to the spiritual life in terms of thinking of self too much in prayer, becoming preoccupied with where we are on the spiritual journey, seeking spiritual experiences, or not being honest with ourselves about our weaknesses and self-deceptions. In short, we easily center on self. Let all this self-focus be swept away in the nothingness.

When you see yourself overly self-centered, accept nothingness. Accept the nothingness of your failure to be un-self-centered and let this widen into accepting the divine nothingness. And let this happen all in the moment. Do not bother about yourself or about what others think of you. Do not be concerned with how you look to others, or with how others perceive you. Do not give any attention to your *self* at all - except through awareness, through seeing your inner egoic patterns. And, eventually, you will not need self-observation of the ego. You will simply be able to sink into nothingness. Indeed, there will come a point in your journey when the nothingness will not leave. Then, no one can hurt you, not even your greatest enemy: yourself.

We might summarize our daily practice of nothingness with the words of Meister Eckhart's definition of spiritual poverty as *wanting nothing, knowing nothing, and having nothing.*[91] This description holds a rich spiritual insight and wisdom for our contemporary life: being happy with nothing. Spiritual poverty exults in nothing: nothing but God, nothing but the nothing who is your deepest self. Being happy with nothing means 1) being happy not having any things, 2) being happy in the nothingness and emptiness of the present moment, 3) being happy in the nothingness of silence and solitude, 4) being happy with the nothingness of routine, 5) being happy with the nothingness of unknowing, 6) being happy within the nothingness of paradox and tension, 7) being happy with others as they are, 8) being happy with what is, with reality as it is right here and right

---

[91] *Meister Eckhart: Essential Sermons*, 199

now, and 9) being happy with the nothing beyond nothing of God and self. Being happy with nothing is all about letting distinction vanish and letting oneness reign.

To unpack the practice of nothingness, I will examine the application of the practice in two real life situations: traffic and boredom. For most people, it takes no effort to imagine being stuck in traffic. You are on your way home, when you forget there's construction in the freeway. The workers have shut down two lanes, and there are cars and trucks backed up for miles. Your expected travel time has tripled. How does this make you feel? Typically, I feel frustrated. In my mind, I tick off a list of people and institutions I'd like to harangue: the construction workers, the people who planned it, the initial people who built the highway, all the other cars on the road. No one escapes my wrath! What goes on within you as you sit in traffic?

Now, apply the practice of nothingness: let everything be reduced to nothing; let your mind come to rest in nothingness. Let all the feelings I just described - as well as any others that come up - to pass through you without clinging to them, without identifying with them. At anytime during the experience of being stuck in traffic you can do this. If it is helpful, take a few deep breaths to ease your mind into nothingness, or return to your sacred word and let that lead you into the state of interior nothingness. Immediately, you can sense freedom coming alive in the form of a space. A bit of space between your feelings and what to do with them develops. Usually it is an experience of a knee-jerk reaction, that is, we identify with our feelings to such a degree that we instantly act them out. In the case of traffic we might curse, bang on the steering wheel, complain, or call to mind all the people we'd like to yell at. Acting from the mystical nothingness, though, lets that space develop between the event and our reaction to it, which allows us to replace our reaction with a chosen response. For instance, I decided not to complain, and see the traffic as an opportunity to rest in God's presence.

We can repeat the dynamic of allowing nothingness into a daily life circumstance anywhere and anytime: at the grocery store, at work, with family, walking in a park, or sipping a latte at Starbucks. So, I will relate the practice to one more example from real life: boredom. We can feel bored in a variety of circumstances. There is so much in our culture that tries to ward off boredom and keep us entertained for as long as possible. The next time you feel bored, however, I invite you to attempt the practice of nothingness. Boredom acts like any other feeling, whether it is anger or sadness or happiness. It will arise and it will disappear on its own. So, to practice nothingness with the experience of boredom, don't do anything! In other words, do not immediately try to get rid of boredom by plugging in to any number of devices: smartphone, tablet, laptop, desktop, television, or radio. Stay unplugged. And, even more, keep your mind unplugged. Settle into the nothingness within. Of course, the feeling of boredom may hang around, too. Let it. Let your focus, your concern, be the mystery of God. Take an experience of boredom as an opportunity to enjoy God, and let everything else be reduced to nothing - including the preoccupation with driving away boredom, or the need to be entertained.

As you can see, the practice of nothingness has the potential for an incredible transformation. Most of this little book has been concerned with conversion and spiritual change on the personal level. Divine love, though, challenges us to move beyond just the personal side of transformation. God desires love, mercy, peace, and justice to cover the whole earth! So, we move to explore a few reflections on the relationship between the practice of nothingness and social transformation.

In the introduction, I mentioned that I do not want to allow mystical nothingness to be interpreted in such a way that it furthers the oppression of groups who are poor, abused, or suffering in any way. In other words, nothingness needs a connection to justice and Gospel-based movements towards liberation. I am referring to justice regarding the poor, women, minorities, the natural world, anyone who is not free. Mystical nothingness proclaims: If God is not an object, people are not objects, creation is not an object. Objectification creates situations of injustice.

The practice of nothingness directly confronts persons and institutions solidifying their own interests at the expense of marginal groups. It does so, first of all, by prophetically critiquing the idolatrous nature of "the system." By "the system" I mean the morass of political, economic, and social conditions that works for the benefit of the rich and to the detriment of the poor and marginal. "Neoliberalism" is a good descriptor of what I mean.

> Neoliberalism is the defining political economic paradigm of our time - it refers to the policies and processes whereby a relative handful of private interests are permitted to control as much as possible of social life in order to maximize their personal profit. Associated initially with Reagan and Thatcher,...neoliberalism has been the dominant global political economic trend adopted by political parties of the center and much of the traditional left as well as the right. These parties and the policies they enact represent the immediate interests

of extremely wealthy investors and less than one thousand large corporations.[92]

Others call it, simply, money-theism.[93] It is the full-on worship of the "Almighty Dollar." The powerful make decisions affecting billions from the perspective of what will earn them more money, completely disregarding the inherent dignity of whole swaths of people. In this situation, the practice of nothingness means first stripping ourselves of such an outlook. It means letting go of economic interest as the only motivating factor in life.

Moreover, the practice of nothingness functions as a call to topple the evils of the system, to annihilate them in favor of more just and compassionate guiding principles. This annihilation is identical to the smashing of idols, to Jesus driving the money changers out of the temple. For, the God we worship is the God we become. If we worship the economic God, everything we see will be in terms of profit. Whereas, if we worship the God who is nothingness, love, and compassion we will not allow any THING to take God's place and see the world through the eyes of divine mercy.

With divine mercy as the guide, the practice of nothingness then challenges us to take the side of the marginal and poor in compassionate solidarity. Whether it is women, African-Americans, the Gay community, or the poor of any nation, God asks us to join them. God invites us to take their side, listen to them, and work with them for just and equal rights. To do so requires a great degree of self-annihilation, especially if we are among the in-group: white,

---

[92] McChesney, Robert W., "Introduction," *Profit Over People: Neoliberalism and Global Order*, NY: Seven Stories Press, 1999. Kindle Edition.
[93] Groody, Daniel G., *Globalization, Spirituality, and Justice*, NY: Orbis Books, 2007. Kindle Edition, ch.1.

males, American (or maybe also European), and rich. Such people must give special attention to letting themselves become nothing so as to join God in raising up those who - unjustly - have been brought low.

Beyond social activism, though, the practice of nothingness holds a special invitation regarding the practice of social justice: *do nothing*. Practice non-cooperation with evil. Do not resist with violence, but with nothingness. Jesus says, "Do not resist the evil-doer." He also provides a warrant for the practice of nothingness as a liberative practice in the parable of the ten gold coins:

> While they were listening to him speak, he proceeded to tell a parable because he was near Jerusalem and they thought that the kingdom of God would appear there immediately. So he said, "A nobleman went off to a distant country to obtain the kingship for himself and then to return. He called ten of his servants and gave them ten gold coins and told them, 'Engage in trade with these until I return.' His fellow citizens, however, despised him and sent a delegation after him to announce, 'We do not want this man to be our king.' But when he returned after obtaining the kingship, he had the servants called, to whom he had given the money, to learn what they had gained by trading. The first came forward and said, 'Sir, your gold coin has earned ten additional ones.' He replied, 'Well done, good servant! You have been faithful in this very small matter; take charge of ten cities.' Then the second came and reported, 'Your gold coin, sir, has earned five more.' And to this servant too he said, 'You, take charge of five cities.' Then the other servant came and said, 'Sir, here is your gold coin; I kept it stored away in a

handkerchief, for I was afraid of you, because you are a demanding person; you take up what you did not lay down and you harvest what you did not plant.' He said to him, 'With your own words I shall condemn you, you wicked servant. You knew I was a demanding person, taking up what I did not lay down and harvesting what I did not plant; why did you not put my money in a bank? Then on my return I would have collected it with interest.' And to those standing by he said, 'Take the gold coin from him and give it to the servant who has ten.' But they said to him, 'Sir, he has ten gold coins.' 'I tell you, to everyone who has, more will be given, but from the one who has not, even what he has will be taken away. Now as for those enemies of mine who did not want me as their king, bring them here and slay them before me.'" (Luke 19:11-27)

The parable depicts a wicked king who steals money he did not invest and plunders harvests he did not plant. It is a parable about unfettered greed, for the king praises the servants who made him money. But, he punishes the third servant for not doing so. His final statement amounts to our saying about the rich getting richer and the poor getting poorer. Greed is rewarded. Resistance to greed and unjust economic practices is punished.

The third servant perfectly depicts the stance of a poor one, a nothing, who stands against unjust authority – both political and economic. The third servant does nothing with the coin. He knew the king was unjust – *a demanding person, taking up what he did not lay down and harvesting what he did not plant* – and he responds by refusing the whole dirty rotten system. He resists injustice by the practice of nothing, which, paradoxically, empowers him to speak truth to power. The servant takes quite a risk, knowing the king freely deals out death to his opponents. But, the nothingness gives us power: we need nothing to be happy and we can recognize when those who think they are something attempt to oppress, manipulate, and dominate others. The nothingness gives us sight, sight to see through the lies and illusions of the system, "mammon." Even though we may feel afraid - as the servant feels toward the wicked king - we can find hope and courage in the nothing. We find the fearlessness born of faith in the mercy and the mystery of God

Thus, the practice of nothingness extends beyond the borders of meditation time. It can infect our whole day with an attitude of letting go into God, freedom from attachments, and inform our commitment to justice. It can serve the transformation of self and society.

# Chapter 6

## The Experience of Failure in the Contemplative Life

Now, I would like to look at a particularly poignant set of experiences that come along in the journey of a contemplative: failure, weakness, and sin. Often, we can feel like we've failed in the spiritual journey, especially when we catch ourselves being selfish or petty or closed-minded. At certain times, it can feel like we're going backwards. It can feel like we're going nowhere. Nothing ever seems to happen in prayer. Here is a special meaning of nothingness. When our prayer is nothing we can feel like nothing is happening in the sense that we are failing at doing it right, or that God is failing us by being absent or forgetful of us. We could even conclude that God does not exist at all. Each one of us can ask, why hasn't this spiritual experience happened? Why am I still attached to so many things? Why do I still do sinful things? Why is my prayer time so boring and lifeless? Why don't I feel closer to God? In my practice of centering prayer I feel like I've been thinking my thoughts the whole time, so what's the point of doing this practice? In general each one of us can feel like our efforts are fruitless and centering prayer is not delivering on its promise of greater freedom, joy, peace, or whatever else we expected.

Experiencing failure on the contemplative path can open us to self-knowledge, which can be quite humbling. Our response to self-knowledge, in fact, can lead to greater growth or keep us imprisoned in ego. For, once we feel our weakness, we often get hooked in a cycle of self-hatred and self-judgment that is not only unnecessary, but also painful and an obstacle to divine love pouring through us. God does not leave us there, however. God orchestrates countless opportunities to trust in the divine mercy and so open at ever-deepening levels to the mystery of the divine nothing.

To break open our experience of failure and meet it with the teaching on nothingness, let's examine three pieces of scripture: Jesus' parable of the barren fig tree in Luke's Gospel, Paul's report of his thorn in the flesh in the Second Letter to the Corinthians, and the parable of the weeds and the wheat in the Gospel of Matthew. These scriptures will help us understand the experience of failure along the contemplative journey.

First, let us inspect the parable of the barren fig tree as well as Thomas Keating's reflection on it. Here is the parable from the Gospel of Luke:

> There once was a person who had a fig tree planted in his orchard, and when he came in search of fruit on it but found none, he said to the gardener, 'For three years now I have come in search of fruit on this fig tree but have found none. (So) cut it down. Why should it exhaust the soil?' He said to him in reply, 'Sir, leave it for this year also, and I shall cultivate the ground around it and fertilize it; it may bear fruit in the future. If not you can cut it down.' (Luke 13:6-9)

Thomas Keating offers the following comments on the parable of the barren fig tree:

> What are we left with at the conclusion of this parable? A tree that is good for nothing. The gardener offers to shovel manure around it, but there is no indication that any new growth will actually occur. This tree and its predicament are striking symbols of daily life, especially when our

efforts to do good fail or seem to be fruitless, our prayer periods are as dry as dust, and nothing ever happens. In addition, there is no sense of God's presence in daily life, no enlightenment experience, while our faults continue, people blame us unjustly, and disappointments multiply. Our spiritual life seems to be dead. What are we to do? The parable seems to say, just keep waiting.[94]

The barren fig tree represents our experience on the contemplative journey: we can sometimes feel stuck, sterile, and hopeless. Keating then says this:

> The parable hints that it does not matter if we do not succeed in our own estimation or in that of others. The divine presence is so present that nothing can take it from us...When we realize the fact of God's closeness, success and failure are relativized. We simply do what we can: that is, throw a little manure--symbol of our fruitless efforts--on the old stick. Of course it is not going to grow, because it is dead. But in some mysterious way, because of God's solidarity with us in everyday life, something much more important happens.[95]

We can poignantly feel our weakness. But, that is precisely where God may want us. God is always one with us - even and especially in our weakness. God may be giving us exactly what we need to grow. The tree receives help from the gardener in the form of manure! Often we have to receive what we would rather not receive, but which, in fact,

---

[94] Keating, Thomas, *Meditations on the Parables of Jesus*, NY: Crossroad, 2010, 42-43.
[95] *Ibid.*, 43

turns out to be best for us. And, humbly bearing our faults, though it may feel like a heap of manure, may be one of the noblest things we can do in our lives.

> The experience of failure can cause no little disappointment and disillusionment. But disappointment in what is the question we have to ask. The answer is usually to be found in our deep-seated expectations, of course. Divine love is not normally going to change the situation by some great miracle. It is trying to change us, so that we can courageously and lovingly unite ourselves to God in the situation.[96]

In other words, God wants, first, to change our expectations and assumptions before going to work on other issues. Often, these are more harmful to us than our mistakes or behaviors we perceive as sinful. God knows we need certain experiences to help us break out of our egos. Even great saints need these experiences. Saint Paul is one of them. In his Second Letter to the Corinthians he reports one of these experience, which he calls a "thorn in the flesh":

> Therefore, that I might not become too elated, a thorn in the flesh was given to me, an angel of Satan, to beat me, to keep me from being too elated. Three times I begged the Lord about this, that it might leave me, but he said to me, 'My grace is sufficient for you, for power is made perfect in weakness.' I will rather boast most gladly of my weaknesses, in order that the power of Christ may dwell with me. Therefore, I am content with weaknesses, insults, hardships, persecutions, and

---

[96] *Ibid.*, 47

constraints, for the sake of Christ; for when I am weak, then I am strong. (2 Cor.12:7-10)

Paul received a thorn in the flesh, a weakness to bear, to descend into humility and not ascend into pride. But, Paul didn't want it! He wanted God to remove it from his life. Who cannot sympathize with Paul, here? Don't we want our weaknesses removed? Don't we long to have our failures banished from our lives? Yet, the ultimate reason for his weakness is to learn trust in divine mercy. God tells him, "my grace is enough for you, for power is made perfect in weakness." True power develops only in the context of weakness and failure. When we are weak – nothing – we are truly powerful. Note that Paul says he is "content with weaknesses." The point here is we can be happy with nothing. We can be happy amidst our various experiences of failure, weakness, and even sin. This is real power. Then nothing can harm us! And, note why. Paul suffers these experiences "for Christ." This indicates his trust in God and his commitment to the way of Jesus: the way of nothingness. This is the way of the crucified.

He realizes that to be weak is to be strong: "when I am weak, then I am strong." Weakness is not an end in and of itself. Rater, the end is the power and strength of Christ. And, we receive this tremendous power in faith. So, remember, the point is not to succumb to despair because we don't feel perfect or holy. Indeed, our weakness is part and parcel of our contemplative experience. The point is to trust in divine mercy by allowing nihil.

Let us round out our exploration into the Bible with a final parable. This one is from chapter thirteen of Matthew's Gospel:

> He proposed another parable to them. "The kingdom of heaven may be likened to a man who

sowed good seed in his field. While everyone was asleep his enemy came and sowed weeds all through the wheat, and then went off. When the crop grew and bore fruit, the weeds appeared as well. The slaves of the householder came to him and said, 'Master, did you not sow good seed in your field? Where have the weeds come from?' He answered, 'An enemy has done this.' His slaves said to him, 'Do you want us to go and pull them up?' He replied, 'No, if you pull up the weeds you might uproot the wheat along with them. Let them grow together until harvest; then at harvest time I will say to the harvesters, "First collect the weeds and tie them in bundles for burning; but gather the wheat into my barn."' (Matt.13:24-30)

"Let them grow together." The householder offers sage advice for the spiritual life. We cannot root out our inner evils without doing more harm than good. This refers to our efforts to get rid of our faults and failings. To do this is to do violence to ourselves. And, whatever we resist we give more power to. We make our sins stronger. Allowing our sins and weaknesses to remain may seem like a bad idea, but there comes a point in the spiritual life when we cannot do anymore and only God will be able to root out sin completely. Hence, it is only at harvest time (the end of the parable) that the weeds and wheat are separated. Removing our faults is God's business. Our business is the humble acceptance of ourselves as we are, which is precisely how God removes our faults and transforms us – the divine acceptance of us.

These three selections from scripture all reveal what we may never know otherwise: God uses our weakness to our benefit, for transformation. This is a fundamental message of the cross. Keating connects the parable of the barren fig tree with Jesus' experience on the cross:

> The divine emptiness of Jesus (in his abandonment by God—'My God, my God, why have you forsaken me?') is the point of God's saving mercy. We experience the same divine emptiness in our daily lives as we wait for something to happen that will fix everything that seems wrong in our particular environment or in us. Jesus in the parables affirms, 'The kingdom is right where you are with your bundle of difficulties, your sense of getting nowhere and waiting in prayer for experiences that never happen.' Divine union is not the achievement of some perfection of our own or an escape from external problems, but is the radical change of attitudes that enables us to deal effectively with our weaknesses and our problems-- the humble acceptance of our lives just as they are, including the monumental moral corruption we may find in ourselves.[97]

So, we will often have a daily experience of nothingness, of our own felt lack of growth, a feeling that we may be going backwards, or just the experience of our much-hated weaknesses. Yet, it is precisely in this nothingness that we can identify with Christ crucified. Just as he encountered the divine nothing in his abandonment on the cross, we can also. For, in Jesus Christ Crucified, God has entered into humanity's lowest point, our worst moments, and our own deepest sin. God has revealed that our nothingness *is* the divine nothingness. Humble acceptance of ourselves as we

---

[97] *Ibid.*, 46-47

are is the point of entry into our own nothingness as well as God's.

So, the cross is the source of spiritual negation. It includes all the negativity God uses to transform us. In weakness, failure, losing, confusion, poverty, stupidity, and oppression we are predisposed to opening to God in Christ through the Spirit because all these experiences are a share in the crucifixion. This is the reversal Jesus proclaims in his parables of God's reign. The last shall be first. The first are those whose lives are so together they do not see the need for God. They do not realize where ultimate happiness lies. They are under illusion and the only way to break them of this illusion is to actually break them open through participation in Christ's passion and death on the cross. But, the last are those already crushed, marginalized, and oppressed. These last ones can be the poor of the third world, all who experience the evils of racism, women suffering from the evils of sexism, the depressed, the socially awkward, the disabled, prisoners, the elderly - the list goes on and on. All of them are crucified. And being in such a position has a spiritual advantage. They are already broken open and can more easily come to know they need God.

God, in fact, does use these people and these experiences to change the rest of us. And it will most definitely be experienced as an annihilation: "God chose the foolish of the world to shame the wise, and God chose the weak of the world to shame the strong, and God chose the lowly and despised of the world, those who count for nothing, to reduce to nothing those who are something."(1 Corinthians 1:27-28) Indeed, God wants to reduce all of us to nothing: the divine nothing. For when we are nothing, we are happy. We share in the divine life. This annihilation is a sharing in the crucifixion of Christ. In his commentary on the parable of the barren fig tree, Keating says the following:

What is special about us is God's incredible solidarity with our ordinary lives: with our sense of failure, futility, getting nowhere spiritually, and our lack of inner resources to cope with our particular difficulties. In the parables daily life is so clearly the place where the kingdom is working that symbols of success are totally irrelevant...Trust in God disregards the evidence of everyday life that God is absent or forgetful of us and brings us into direct contact with the God of everyday. The God of pure faith is so close: closer than breathing, closer than thinking, closer than choosing, closer than consciousness itself...An enlightened faith seems very ordinary. One might scarcely notice it. It accepts the way things are and finds God vibrantly present in the most insignificant situations and in the most unexpected disguises. 'Dung' in this parable is the symbol of humble hope, which keeps trusting in God without trying to analyze or resolve the tension between the hard realities of everyday life and God's sovereignty.[98]

Therefore, let failure be an opportunity to return; Let failure be an opportunity for consent. Amidst experiences of failure, selfishness, and sin ever-so-gently return to your sacred symbol. Effortlessly accept your weaknesses. Let experiences of failure and sin disappear into nothing. In moments of sin, ever-so-gently return to your sacred symbol. In moments of sin, confess and effortlessly allow (open to) divine mercy. When you fail or sin effortlessly consent to divine mercy. Gently persevere through experiences of failure and sin.

---

[98] *Ibid.*, 45

Now,. in our practice of centering prayer we often fail. We discover that we are constantly engaging our thoughts. In fact, in nineteen out of twenty minutes of centering prayer we may be totally absorbed in our thinking and our feelings. Truly, to do centering prayer, to meditate, is to journey into failure and a full-throttle experience of our own weakness. We find that we just cannot do it on our own. we cannot make our minds silent. We cannot rest in the nothing. We just cannot do it. This, however, is a great grace from God. For, in seeing our inability and feeling our weakness, we simultaneously realize divine mercy. When we cannot do it right, or when we just plain fail we can rejoice for then we can surrender to God's mercy in the silence and nothingness (or lack thereof!) of our centering prayer. The experience of failure is a great grace because it helps us let go of our attachment to control and to maintaining a separate, independent self. Simply put, experiencing our weakness helps us to surrender to divine mercy and let go of our prideful egos who think they can do it all on their own.

This, however, does not dispense us from living moral lives. We do our best in that regard. But, it does mean we should not lose heart when we experience our failure and sin - especially when we experience them *often*. In discovering divine mercy amidst our failures - particularly when we fail at the method of centering prayer - we learn to accept ourselves as God accepts us. We learn to accept ourselves just as we are and with gratuitous love.

In all these experiences we experience the mercy of God in a deeper way. We experience God reducing us to nothing in the divine nothing. And, here is the good news: it is all God's mercy! Through letting us fail God is giving us an opportunity to surrender, to let our very selves become nothing. An instance of failure or sin provides us with at least two choices: despair that we are not yet perfect or hope that God's mercy embraces us. To choose despair is to choose self. To choose hope in divine mercy is to choose to surrender the ego's tight grip on the practice of the spiritual journey and let God be in charge. The failure we experience in meditating is the failure of the ego, and it is necessary. The ego needs to fail and we need to experience it so we can yield to the mystery of divine mercy.

More deeply, when we feel our weakness, our failure, our sin, just let nothing. Without effort, without trying, without judgment, allow divine mercy. Accept God on God's terms: humbly and with hearts wide open. We cannot escape our weakness. Our struggles, failures, and sins may never leave us. Instead, we learn humility amidst these experiences. When we experience our failure, we graciously accept God in it. By doing so we become nothing: lesser and lower. And as Jesus says, "the one who is least among all of you is the one who is the greatest." (Luke 9:48)

Apply these insights directly to your experience of centering prayer. When you notice you've been thinking about your thoughts for most of the prayer period, allow merciful nothing. In fact, while centering, let the attempt to "get somewhere" in prayer release itself. "Trying to get somewhere" reflects perfectionism, ego, and self-reference more than contemplative love and nothingness. So, no matter what you experience in prayer, whether it is a barrage of thoughts or constant struggle, *effortless nothing*. Gently persevere through experiences of being preoccupied with thinking. And, when you notice you've been thinking about your thoughts for most of the prayer period, sink into nothing.

God turns death into resurrection. God uses our sin and weakness in our favor, to transform us. We can feel like nothing is happening, like we're not changing, especially because we keep doing the same old addictive behaviors! Still, God uses all of it to change us. All we have to do is let God do it! We are called to trust in divine mercy and return to God. We repent by turning our simple presence back to God. In other words, we surrender. We surrender our sinful behavior, our inability to do anything about it, our awful self-expectations and our imprisoning notions of perfection. Surrender all of it and let God make you new!

It is only in experiences of losing and failure that we realize how utterly dependent, fragile, and weak we are. It is those moments that are a potential sharing in the crucifixion of Christ. Jesus tells us to rejoice in those moments because it is another opportunity for transformation. And we don't need to seek them out because life throws these curve balls at us all the time. Suffocating boredom, intense loneliness, those moments when life simply falls apart—rejoice in these moments because it is in them that God frees us. It is in these moments that we learn to fall into the mystery of God. God is found in the most painful, sinful, uncomfortable, and negative experiences of life. That's what the cross says! And, we would never expect to find God there. True life comes through death journeys wherein we realize who God is for us: the God of liberating, gratuitous, mysterious love. In our little deaths we become nothing. We become nothing with Christ crucified. We die with Christ. We die with, through, and in God. We realize we are nothing, just as Christ Crucified is nothing, just as God is nothing.

## Chapter 7

## The Hiddenness of Contemplation

Self-knowledge is among the first fruits of contemplative prayer. And, often, it will not feel like a gift. It will feel like we are getting worse, like we are going backwards. In other words, growth in contemplative prayer will be experienced as a lack of growth. An acute experience, then, of the mature contemplative is that we do not seem to be changing or getting any better. Our twenty to thirty minutes of centering prayer feels lifeless, dull, routine, and it is as if God is nowhere to be seen. God has, it seems, abandoned us - whether all at once or gradually over time. God has vanished from our experience. What are we to do? *Nothing*, as I am sure you could have guessed! Yes, at this point we are entering into nothingness on a deeper level. This is an event in the life of a contemplative that will test faith.

Now, our culture tends to think, and therefore we tend to think, that we can experience God like we can experience anything in the world. So, our God-experience must be just like our experience of a chair, or a picture, or even a person. While there may be some similarities, especially with experiencing a person, God far transcends this. God is not one more object of experience in the world. God is not an object at all.

Experience includes the senses, our feelings, and our interpretations of the "moment" of experience. For example, we can experience a painting in the following manner: there is our immediate contact with the painting by sight, then the feelings it stirs up in us (maybe interest or boredom), and finally we formulate an opinion or interpretation of the event such as "I love this painting" or "I'm not too thrilled by it." These interpretations are often self-reflections. Sometimes we assume meeting God happens in just the same manner. So, we presume we can sense God, feel God, and interpret God. But, again, God is mystery beyond experience. As Keating says in *Invitation to Love*:

> The tendency to identify contemplative prayer with felt experience is very deeply ingrained in us, however - and, unfortunately, it keeps getting reinforced. There has been a tendency among spiritual writers in recent centuries to identify contemplation with the felt presence of God…In textbooks dealing with spiritual theology, we find the assumption, either stated or presupposed, that contemplation must be felt to be real.[99]

Experiences can keep us self-preoccupied. After all, it is the self who is the one having the experience. In particular, we can become overly centered on ourselves when we try to determine where we are on the spiritual journey. As Keating just alluded to, often spiritual authors of the past have given the impression that experiences are the signs of growth on the spiritual journey. According to Teresa of Avila, the spiritual journey is composed of stages of experiential prayer: the prayer of quiet, the prayer of union, the prayer of full union. Moreover, according to John of the Cross, there are at least two great transitions: the night of sense and the night of spirit, in which God purifies us to a great degree of all selfishness and sin. We can easily read their reflections on the stages and transitions along the spiritual journey and presume that since the experiences they

---

[99] Keating, Thomas, *Invitation to Love: The Way of Christian Contemplation*, NY: Continuum, 1998, 116-117.

describe are nowhere to be seen in our lives, we are not making any progress at all.

Another problem with experiencing God is that we can become attached to anything. We can turn anything into an idol, a false god to worship over the real God. One of the most subtle things we can get hooked is a spiritual experience. We can literally crave spiritual experiences of peace, joy, freedom, God's closeness, and even the feeling of silence and nothingness. Moreover, attachment to spiritual experience can also manifest as resistance to difficult experiences and/or emotions. Frenette reminds us, "centering prayer is not focused on any one spiritual experience, but on letting all experiences go and on letting all experiences be without even trying to let them go."[100]

Thanks be to God that in our centering prayer, more often than not, we experience ourselves and nothing of God. For the apophatic mystics, the encounter with God is primarily characterized by no experience, by the vacuity of experience. God is found in the negation of experience as the nothingness beyond experience, who remains accessible in our experience but is not identified with our experience. God cannot be the "object" of any consciousness whatsoever. The nothingness is not some*thing* to experience, rather "it" transcends experience. Further, any experience we have of God is our interpretation of the divine mystery, because we always bring our own biases, prejudices, feelings, and ideas to any experience. A lot of stuff can get between us and God when we have a spiritual experience. God, thankfully, transcends all our limitations, biases, and blindnesses. So, not to have experiences of God may be a great grace, a great transformation from being focused on oneself to being focused on God alone. Indeed, we may be kept in the dark all through our spiritual journey, which means we may never

---

[100] Frenette, 73

experience the stages of prayer or even the nights of sense and spirit as the mystics describe them. The entire journey may be hidden from us.

Because God transcends thinking, feeling, and experience, we must walk by faith. We may feel like we are not growing, but faith contradicts this feeling and puts it in proper perspective. For, the journey to God is on the road of faith. Keating says, "What is the essence of contemplative prayer? The way of pure faith. Nothing else. You do not have to feel it, but you have to practice it."[101] It is the essence of contemplation because faith is unknowing, knowing beyond the mind by knowing nothing. Faith is knowing nothing.

Let us briefly turn to what John of the Cross declares about faith in the treatises *The Ascent of Mount Carmel* and *The Dark Night of the Soul* to explore the meaning of faith. In these works John says faith is a journey: "Now this road is faith, and for the intellect faith is also like a dark night."[102] John calls faith dark, pure, naked to bring out how God drives us through a conceptual purification. This conceptual purification of faith corresponds to the erasure of all images and ideas of God, even those hallowed by tradition and one's own experience: "However impressive may be one's knowledge or experience of God, that knowledge or experience will have no resemblance to God and amount to very little."[103] The vital purification of faith matches up with our liberation from our deeply ingrained selfish attitudes and expectations regarding who we are, who God is, and how God should act. This vital purification of faith leads the human person into experiences of divine absence and even the feeling of rejection by God: the soul "feels very vividly indeed the shadow of death, the sighs of death, and the

---

[101] Keating, *Open Mind, Open Heart*, 139
[102] *The Collected Works of St. John of the Cross*, 120
[103] *Ibid.*, 160

sorrows of hell, all of which reflect the feeling of God's absence."[104] Through these two dimensions of the night of faith God frees us from all that blocks true relationship with the divine so we may realize oneness. We must lean on nothing but faith for God frees our intellect in this way: "To be prepared for this divine union the intellect must be cleansed and emptied of everything relating to sense, divested and liberated of everything clearly intelligible, inwardly pacified and silenced, and supported by faith alone."[105]

John equates faith with darkness, night, and unknowing. As such, faith is the subjective correlative to the objective mystery of God: the Divine Darkness who is totally Unknown. Faith takes us beyond the mind because God transcends the mind. Pure, dark, unadulterated faith receives God as God - not God as we would like God to be, not information about God, but God as God actually is. And this God is absolutely transcendent mystery who loves us gratuitously. By pure faith we encounter the hidden and living triune God. Therefore, the heart of the Christian mystical journey to divine oneness is faith because it purifies us of all our concepts, images, and expectations regarding God. God leads us into the unknowing of faith to free us from limited and narrow ways of relating to the divine and to open us evermore to the gift of divine love.

Recall that John says our experiences of God will never grasp the reality of God. In other words, our experiences of God are just that, experiences. What matters is staying centered on God and not our experiences of God. This is a subtle distinction, but necessary because our capacity for addiction and idolatry is enormous. We can become addicted to religious experiences, images, ideas, and feelings just as

---

[104] *Ibid.*, 404
[105] *Ibid.*, 177

much as we can become addicted to drugs or alcohol. John's way of pure faith keeps our eyes on the prize, God, and not on experiences. Many ordinary Christians assume a close relationship with God - being a mystic - means having revelations, visions, locutions, etc. They presume holiness is based on particular religious experiences. Not so, according to John. Pure faith is the heart of the journey and constitutes holiness. Often God speaks in silence and does not give us exalted experiences because God wants us to love Godself and not God's gifts.

Faith, according to John, challenges us to let God be God. For John, we come to know God as God, not God as we would like, in the darkness and unknowing of faith. The challenge John presents to us is to let God be who God is and not to project our own concepts, ideas, and expectations onto God. Cooperating with God as God leads us into the unknowing of faith and means letting our ideas of God fall away to give God the chance to introduce Godself. Keating says, "Pure faith transcends every human experience and accesses God just as God is."[106]

This also entails letting God act as God would act. Such a challenge calls for our trust in God's providential guidance. John presents the way of pure faith as a being led by the Divine Spirit into the wholly mysterious and unknown. To let God be God and act as God acts, then, is incredibly risky! It de-centers us because letting God be God means we cannot be God! We must let go of control, security, our expectations, and agendas so the sole agenda becomes the reign of God.

Thus, for John of the Cross, faith is a journey into darkness and unknowing, which corresponds to the darkness and unknowability of God, the divine nothingness. Moreover, the darkness and unknowing of faith into which

---

[106] Keating, *Invitation to Love*, 117

God leads us relativizes our religious experiences and calls us to let go of ourselves to let God be God - the nothing. John knows that nothing short of the absolute mystery of God will satisfy the human heart. He is, therefore, uncompromising. He advises us not to settle for our knowledge, our experience, or our images but to surrender to God in the nothingness and unknowing of faith.

Pure Faith is faith that rests on no props. It is simple surrender to God in darkness and unknowing. Leaving behind all thoughts, feelings, and perceptions, we give ourselves to God. We do this because God is mystery and cannot be reduced to our ideas or concepts. It is absolute and unconditional trust in divine goodness, without the help of feelings of consolation or even a sign that gives us a hint of reassurance. It is the total gift of ourselves to God beyond all reason and all experience. It works like this:

> The deeper our prayer actually is, the more it habitually drops out of our ordinary awareness...The subtler and more spiritual the experience of grace, the less we perceive it...Thus deep rest can be present in prayer, but its source is on such a high frequency that it is no longer translated as rest or consolation. There is simply a mysterious attraction and hunger for God.[107]

Applied to our prayer lives, pure faith means to simply remain faithful to our contemplative practice even and especially when it feels like we are going nowhere. First, Keating:

> The way of pure faith is to persevere in contemplative practice without worrying about

---

[107] Keating, *Intimacy with God*, NY: Crossroad, 2009, 68-69.

> where we are on the journey, and without comparing ourselves with others or judging others' gifts as better than ours. We can be spared all this nonsense if we surrender ourselves to the divine action, whatever the psychological content of our prayer may be. In pure faith, the results are often hidden even from those who are growing the most.[108]

Now, consider Frenette:

> What does pure faith mean, practically? It means to continue in the ordinariness, the dryness, the emptiness of your daily contemplative practice…Let nada, nothing, become toda, the source of everything.[109]

Our discussion so far shows that even though many people don't have mystical experiences or even know they are going through transition points or markers on the journey, it is okay. Their own spiritual progress is hidden or secret from them. Often, these same people don't even care that they don't seem to be making any "progress." This is a wonderful sign of self-forgetfulness. Their centering is what it is. They don't judge their centering. They don't try to make their centering into anything or any expected result or any spiritual experience.

So, there is a connection here to the hidden life of contemplation. Most contemplatives realize divine oneness without knowing it. They aren't even aware they're being non-reflective. Self-forgetfulness is not self-conscious. Full oneness has no thought; there is no reflection of self. The

---

[108] Keating, *Invitation to Love*, 118
[109] Frenette, 88

ability to be happy even though you don't seem to be growing or "making any spiritual progress" could be a good sign that you are more comfortable with mystery -- with your personal spiritual ambiguity (at least as YOU define it). In other words, this shows the ability to hold the tension of two opposites, holding a paradox. And this is a serious and deep growth in faith. So, this may very well be a sign of greater trust in God amidst your overwhelming failures and mistakes! So, rejoice! "You can tell adult and authentic faith by people's ability to deal with darkness, failure, and nonvalidation of the ego - and by their quiet but confident joy!"[110]

Indeed, the very ability to stick with prayer when it seems fruitless, boring, and sterile is a great sign of deep faith. And, even better, this perseverance is not coming from you! To remain in the nothingness day after day is a gift of God. "No human will is stubborn enough to simply go through these motions. If the endurance is from you, you will inevitably abandon it. If the perseverance is from God, you can never effectively abandon prayer indefinitely."[111]

The nothingness defies our expectations of what transformation may look like in us. The change that comes about through God can be very secret. So, "for many persons, their whole contemplative journey is completely hidden from them until their final transformation."[112] A sure sign of deepening contemplation, then, is that we do not know we are in contemplation. It is hidden from us. Evagrius Ponticus, in his Scholia on Psalm 126.2, says, "Just as when we are asleep we do not know that we sleep, so neither when we are contemplating do we know that we have

---

[110] Rohr, Richard, *The Naked Now*, NY: Crossroad, 2009, 120.
[111] Nemeck, 79-80
[112] Keating, *Open Mind, Open Heart*, 139

passed into contemplation."[113] We are awakening to God within us, but it is not an experience nor even a set of experiences. We wake up without even knowing it. It is un-self-conscious. As I have been saying, it is perfect self-forgetfulness. For, we do not even care whether or not we are deepening our contemplative life. Of course, the full growth of contemplative prayer will still happen in a person, but it "is so pure that it is not perceptible to the one receiving it. It is manifest, however, in the progressive transformation of the person."[114]

Our faith deepens, but we care less and less about where we are on the journey. We may have many experiences that we would think a contemplative would never have to deal with. We may experience multiple conflicting and painful emotions, difficult decisions, and even personal tragedy. The deepening of our faith, of knowing nothing, corresponds exactly to our capacity to hold these tensions in the nothingness instead of imposing our pain on others. In this sense, faith is but keeping ourselves open to God: "Faith is a word that points to an initial opening of the heart space or the mind space from our side...Faith is our small and necessary offering to any new change or encounter."[115]

Faith is an openness on our part to being okay with knowing nothing. And, it manifests in our lives as a deep commitment to the journey, to our daily practice. Faith in practice is fidelity amidst the trials of remaining in the obscure nothingness of God. According to Jesus, such faith

---

[113] Scholia on Psalm 126.2, quoted in Harmless, William, *Desert Christians: An Introduction to the Literature of Early Monasticism*, NY: Oxford University Press, 2004. Kindle Edition, ch.11.
[114] Keating, *Open Mind, Open Heart*, 114
[115] Rohr, *The Naked Now*, 116

is the narrow way that leads to life. So, remain in the nothingness with a pure faith. God will transform us.

But the chances are good that [we ourselves] will not perceive this. Lay people living quiet, prayerful lives in the world, who think they are not contemplatives because they never became monks or nuns, and elderly religious, who think they are not contemplatives...may be so holy that they are not even upset by their apparent failure as contemplatives. This is the triumph of hiddenness.[116]

All in all, the contemplative life is mostly hidden from us. And so, we must patiently wait for transformation in pure faith. In our practice, this means more nothingness. Endure knowing nothing, experiencing nothing. The nothingness defies our expectations of what transformation may look like in us - transformation can be very secret.

Persist in this scattered emptiness. Although our deepest self abides in a peaceful, loving attentiveness towards God, on a conscious level we may experience a veritable irksomeness at the prospect of remaining in the obscurity of faith. Occasionally too, this weariness may even lead the soul to be repelled by the very thought of spending time in solitary prayer. This in turn causes it further distress since the soul so deeply desires to love God and remain in his love.[117]

---

[116] Keating, *Invitation to Love*, 119
[117] Nemeck, 78

An essential feature of the hiddenness of contemplative prayer is that we must "put up with ourselves." In practicing meditation, we suffer ourselves - with our roaming minds, distraction, the burden of self-consciousness, the all-too-quick forays into thinking and judging. What is required of us is patient endurance.

The essence of mysticism is the path of pure faith. Trust and love God beyond what you experience or don't experience, without feeling or even being aware of God. Willingly and patiently endure not knowing where you are on the journey. Accept the poverty and godlessness of your prayer. To do so is to practice nothingness. Ruminate over these phrases: *Silent Nothing; Open Nothing; Singular Nothing; Effortlessly let God be God: nothing. Love God in mindless oblivion. During meditation: mindless oblivion.* When thoughts come let them keep going. If you start thinking a thought, meet it with silence, that is, the mystical void: mindless oblivion. In contemplative prayer, there is only nothingness, the nothingness of non-experience, the divine nothingness. Meet thoughts and feelings with nihility - let the internal dialogue dissolve into nothing. Simply allow non-experiential emptiness.

This is a giving way to the mystery of love, and allowing the void of godless nothing to engulf you. Such prayer leaves behind thoughts, feelings, and experiences of all kinds to be suffused with divinity. It is an exercise in naked faith, a faith that rests on God alone. We may not experience anything. In fact, it will seem like "doing nothing." In this space all will be annihilated and the divine will give itself to you gratuitously and with overwhelming joy. It is the prayer of annihilation in the divine nothing.

## Chapter 8

## Prayer in Secret: Just Nothing

In this, the final chapter, I would like to draw our reflections together under the wisdom saying of Jesus in Matthew 6:6 on prayer in secret. I will interpret this saying as Jesus' teaching on nothingness in contemplative prayer. Then, I will look more closely at the secrecy of nothingness by summarizing and deepening the practical instructions on nothingness in prayer, connecting the nothingness of contemplative prayer to the Paschal Mystery, and peeking at nothingness in relation to the goal of the journey: mystical oneness with God.

*Matthew 6:6*

Jesus' teaching on prayer in secret is set in the context of the Sermon on the Mount and specifically between two other sayings on secrecy. Before the sayings on secrecy, Jesus presents the beatitudes then reinterprets some major points of the law - as in "You have heard that it was said, 'You shall love your neighbor and hate your enemy.' But I say to you, love your enemies."(Matt.5:43) Jesus goes further with a reinterpretation of the three traditional religious practices – practices that Catholics, for instance, rededicate themselves to every Lent. These practices are fasting, almsgiving, and prayer. Jesus then teaches non-idolatry and non-judgment. He calls on us to set our hearts on God alone and to act like God - without judgment and with compassion. He ends the Sermon by noting that the one who does what he teaches builds on a firm foundation. The teachings of Jesus, then, offer a grounding in the very life of God.

Turning our attention to the practices of almsgiving, prayer, and fasting, we note that the main lens through which Jesus understands these religious practices is *secrecy*. He first goes teaches almsgiving in secret: "But when you give alms, do not let your left hand know what your right is doing, so that your almsgiving may be secret. And your Father who sees in secret will repay you."(Matt.6:3) The image of not letting your left hand know what your right hand is doing suggests the transcendence of self-consciousness. He then gives his teaching on prayer in secret, which we will give below. Jesus ends this section by giving his view of fasting: "when you fast, anoint your head and wash your face, so that you may not appear to be fasting, except to your Father who is hidden." (Matt.6.17) Now, the secrecy is translated as "hiddenness." Hidden from what? From self. We are hiding our fasting because we can insert self into anything. We can blow trumpets before giving alms and dress shabbily to announce to the world we are fasting. And we do this all for ego.

So, between these two sayings, Jesus offers his teaching on prayer in secret: "When you pray, go to your inner room, close the door, and pray to your Father in secret. And your Father who is in secret will make you flourish." (Matt.6:6) Let us parse the various phrases in this wisdom saying. First, let us examine the phrase "When you pray." Whenever we set out to pray, to enter into God and speak with God we are to follow these instructions. We could translate this phrase as "When you open to God." Prayer is about opening to God much more than us speaking at God. Right after this verse, Jesus tells the people "not to babble like pagans who think they will be heard because of their many words." So, prayer is not about constant words, constant talking. This is a definite shift. We are used to taking the lead in prayer and supposing the burden is on us to start a conversation. This phrase, however, points out that we already have a relationship with God. We are already one with God and so only need to give our attention to this already given reality. Yet, we do not have to secure this relationship with a multiplicity of words. We do not have to talk God into loving us. We already have God. God is already within us and one with us.

Jesus then says "go to your inner room." Jesus invites us to go within, because God is within. Some Bibles translate "inner room" as "private room." Either way it is a metaphor. According to Keating, the vast majority of Jews in first century Palestine did not have anything like a "private room."[118] Only the rich like King Herod, the High Priest, or Pontius Pilate had areas that were private. Most people had to fit their entire family in a single room! Thus, Jesus' audience would clearly have understood him to mean: go within. Keating further interprets the inner room:

> The inner room as a term is pointing to a spiritual, not a physical location...It means to let go of the ordinary psychological awareness of everyday life with its tumult, noise, worries, and the various commentaries that go on in our heads about people, events, and our emotional reactions to them.[119]

To enter our inner room means to allow our normal thoughts to recede into the background and not give our attention to them. In other words, we ignore the normal psychological content of our minds. For example, we ignore all the commentary, external noise, the daydreams, and the to-do lists. We purposely forget our thoughts and do not connect

---

[118] Keating, *Manifesting God*, 74
[119] *Ibid.*, 74

with them during the time of prayer. The inner room is the first step in praying contemplatively, in letting go of the normal content of our minds and surrendering to God.

So, when we pray, first, we are to go to our inner room. Jesus then says to "close the door" to this inner room. His continuation of the metaphor of a private room suggests a further level of letting go. By entering the inner room we abandon our normal thinking and feeling. Now, Jesus instructs us to void our interior dialogue. He invites us to stop the conversation we have with ourselves all day long. It is this conversation that keeps our addictive thinking going, and keeps self as the central reference point. Keating describes the interior dialogue:

> Of what does the interior dialogue normally consist? It is that discussion we have with ourselves that goes on continuously twenty-four hours a day, in which we evaluate and comment on what is happening with regard to events, people entering and leaving our lives and our emotional reactions to them.[120]

When we pray in the inner room, we bring our self-conversation to a halt. We may experience some frustration that thoughts keep coming and we slip back into our interior dialogue often. But, humbly accepting our weakness is a part of the prayer and its flip side is a generous trust in God's love despite and within our weakness.

Once we have closed the door to our inner room, Jesus calls on us to pray in secret to the Father, to his and your Abba: "Pray to your Father in secret." We have let go of all thinking, at least in intention, and now we can simply rest in God. There is nothing to do. We cannot make prayer in

---

[120] *Ibid.*, 78

secret happen. Total effortlessness characterizes secret prayer. Further, in the secrecy of prayer there is nothing to *be*. We do not have to be anyone to pray to Abba in secret. Recall that Simon Tugwell said only "nobody" can submit to this prayer. This prayer takes place in secret; it IS secrecy. Thus, the self has neither knowledge nor experience of it. So, praying in secret transcends all thinking, all self-reflection. It is the total transcendence and surrender of the self into the nothingness of God. Keating offers these comments:

> Notice the reason for prayer in secret that Jesus implies. If we are to access the God who sees in secret and is in secret, we have to enter into the same kind of secrecy. God is so close that we do not have any faculty to interpret the divine presence. Only pure faith beyond thoughts, feelings, and reflections can access it.[121]

Secrecy is Jesus' metaphor describing the transcendent mystery. The secrecy of God is identical to the mystery of God, transcending all even while God is one with all. Further, God is not only secret from our self - with its thinking and experiences - but also from being itself. Hence, we need faith. Pure faith goes deeper than self to access the mystery of God beyond all thinking, all experience, our very self, and even being itself.

But, Jesus does not end there! When you open to God, go within – deeper than your normal thinking mind, to your inner room, and close the door on your interior dialogue. Then, you are praying in secret, but without your *self*. You are transcending all existence. When this happens, "your Father who is in secret will reward you." Admittedly, the

---

[121] *Ibid.*, 79

word "reward" has the connotation of a business transaction: if we pray in secret there will be a reward. It may seem like prayer in secret is a means to an end or to some reward. It is similar to performing some task or job for a monetary reward. In such a situation, money is our goal, and the job is a means to the goal. If we could go right to the goal, we would!

Prayer in secret, however, truly is its own reward. We pray in secret for no extra goal. So, Keating translates this phrase in the following manner: "your Abba who is in secret will make you flourish." "Pray to God who is in secret, and God who is in secret will reward you," is the usual translation. It really means, "will bring your whole human nature to flourish and bloom."[122] Another way of saying this is that you will become God, too, which is your true nature. This gets at Jesus' meaning better. When we pray in secret we realize oneness with the mystery of God. This is its own reward, for God is our happiness. As we pray in secret, God begins to transform us, from ego-consciousness to God-consciousness, to no-consciousness and beyond into the nothingness. So, God will transform us. Prayer in secret is the prayer of nothingness.

Keeping in mind this exposition of Jesus' wisdom saying on prayer in secret, let us turn to the practical instructions on nothingness I have provided so far, and then allow me to deepen them. According to Jesus, prayer in secret is contemplation without any symbols, without any effort, without any experience, without any self-reflection, without self-awareness, without form, totally hidden from us in unknowing. Therefore, prayer in secret is just *nothing*.

---

[122] http://www.contemplativeoutreach.org/site/News2?page=NewsArticle&id=6221

We handle thoughts, failure, our desire for experiences, our need to know where we are on the journey, our egos, self-consciousness, and even the final form of being with nothingness. In centering prayer, nothingness means non-meditation; so, do not try to meditate. Just nothing: absolute effortlessness, no mind and no self - only the mystery of God who is nothing. Recall that just *being* is still a substance relating to another substance, which is still far too dualistic for the divine mystery. In the nothingness we do not even try to let go of thoughts, simply drop all thinking and allow thoughts to pass by with no effort to remove them.

Therefore, drop all thinking and relax into nothingness. Let all thinking, all effort, all possessiveness dissolve into nothing. Let go of all thinking and permit nothingness. Let nothingness surface from deep within you. Let nothing: effortless nothing, sheer nothing, non-thinking nothingness. This is, simply, very simply, nothing. Allow nothingness to replace your efforts and thoughts and feelings: your very self. Allow all your thinking to dissolve into nothing, and remain there in the nothing. You will be highly alert but not thinking.

Just nothing: prayer in secret, which means a lack of content, activity, and self, nothing to do, nothing to be, utterly naked and nondual faith. Contemplative blankness is empty in pure negation. We pray in nothingness because God's presence is no thing, beyond being, nothing. As we praying with, in, and as nothingness God annihilates all dualistic awareness - all awareness - because God annihilates the self. The subject-object division of the mind collapses and disappears. Prayer in secret is about identifying with the absolute nothingness until who we think we are passes away and our identity as the nothingness surfaces - identity not only beyond the ego but also beyond the self.

In the nothingness we are not projecting our thinking, images, or ideas onto God. Instead, we are giving God the chance to introduce the divine mystery as the nothingness beyond being. So, effortlessly let God be God: nothing. It is this nothingness with which we are identifying in contemplative prayer. Let your identity be the same as the nothing. Let the nothingness awaken as you. For, divine nothingness is my nothingness; my nothingness is divine nothingness. In a contemplative manner, savor these phrases: *vanish into nothing; sheer nothing; just nothing; effortless nothing; let nothing; silent nothing; open nothing; happy nothing; merciful nothing; non-thinking nothing; non-reflective nothing; selfless nothing; singular nothing; divine nothing; same nothing.*

Perhaps two parables will help us here. The first is from the Gospel of Thomas. The second is from Thomas Moore's book *Meditations*. In my view, both are parables about the nothingness of contemplative prayer. First, saying 97 from the Gospel of Thomas:

> Jesus said, The [father's] kingdom is like a woman who was carrying a [jar] full of meal. While she was walking along [a] distant road, the handle of the jar broke and the meal spilled behind her [along] the road. She didn't know it; she hadn't noticed a problem. When she reached her house, she put the jar down and discovered that it was empty.[123]

There are two points to note about this parable. First, the woman *did not know* the jar of meal was emptying out behind here. And, second, when she reached her house, *she discovered it was empty*. This saying points to how the reign of God is all about continuous self-emptying or self-annihilation and that the very nature of God is ecstatic

---

[123] *The Gospel of Thomas: The Hidden Sayings of Jesus*, trans. Marvin Meyer, Saying 97, NY: Harper Collins, 1992, 61.

nothingness, dynamic and giving and transcending being - empty. The great spiritual advantage of the nothingness of God, of yourself, and of contemplative prayer is that we cannot *experience* nothingness. If you think you are experiencing nothingness in contemplative prayer, that is not really the nothing but some*thing* you can experience. We can meet, rest in, enjoy, and realize nothingness without experiencing the nothingness, because the nothing is not an object even though to write about the nothing is to make it into an object! The nothingness is present within and beyond whatever you experience in prayer: silence and thoughts, peace and disturbance, rest and restlessness.

Second, here is the parable from Thomas Moore:

> Three monks knelt in the chapel in the dark morning hours before dawn. The first thought he saw the figure of Jesus come down from the cross and rest before him in midair. Finally, he said to himself, I know what contemplation is. The second felt himself rise out of his place in the choir. He soared over his brother monks and surveyed the timber-vaulted ceiling of the church, and then landed back in his place in the choir. I've been blessed, he thought, with a minor miracle, but in humility I must keep it to myself. The third felt his knees growing sore and his legs tired. His minded wandered until it came to a stop on the image of a luscious hamburger laden with pickles and onions. "No matter how hard I try," said the devil's helper to his master, "I can't seem to tempt this third monk."[124]

---

[124] Moore, Thomas, *Meditations: On the Monk Who Dwells in Daily Life*, NY: Harper Collins, 1994, 48.

The point is the third monk did not comment on his thoughts; he let pass his own self-reflection - unlike the other two monks. Moreover, the story relates that true contemplation is not about visions or levitations or any other such special graces. It's about fidelity to nothingness amidst the ordinary wanderings of the mind. Also, contemplative prayer is just ordinary. It's about how we deal with our ordinary thoughts. And the third monk dealt with his thoughts by not attaching to them. This is the way to go! This is practical nothingness!

*The Paschal Mystery*

Just nothing: thoughtless, effortless, experience-less silence. Thoughts float by and you have no interest in them. Consciousness is deeply calm and detached yet still experiencing thoughts and feelings. Sometimes these thoughts are tortuous. Sometimes the mind feels dead. Other time there is a simple letting be and letting nothing. There are many ways to understand these experiences. One, though, is central for Christians: the cross. All of these experiences share in the cross. The cross eminently describes this Christian contemplative prayer. The core, the heart, of Christian contemplation is identifying the Christ Crucified. Our ego, our thoughts, our feelings, our self-conscious, the separate-self-sense are being gradually crucified, let go of, annihilated. But we rarely feel it. Similar to the nihil, a dimension of contemplative prayer that the cross communicates is that we will not feel much at all, that mostly we will not experience anything. We will have to patiently endure or put up with our endless stream of thoughts and feelings. We will have to wait out - in humble trust in God - our very self-consciousness with its constant tendency to possess experiences by reflecting on them. The cross in contemplative practice leads us to resurrection by helping us to humbly accept our seemingly endless thoughts as well as the constant and "oppressive" experience of self-consciousness. In this acceptance lies newness of life.

Prayer in secret, contemplation, is about the gradual identification with the passion, death, and resurrection of Christ. It involves dying to self, or letting go of self. On the cross, God dies to being God. God goes through self-annihilation. This is the supreme revelation of who God is: Absolute Nothingness eternally self-annihilating out of sheer gratuitous love. The crucified Christ reveals God as the nothing. Indeed, when Jesus crucified screams, "My God, my God, why have you abandoned me?", he is expressing the fact that the crucifixion is the death of his ineffable union with the Father in the Spirit. God dies to being God. Yet, because God is ultimate kenosis, or self-emptying / self-annihilation, God transforms Jesus into the Risen Christ. Jesus passes from human subjectivity relating to God into the Divine Subjectivity: identical oneness with infinite nothingness. Keating describes this deeper dimension to the Paschal Mystery:

> Our participation in this Mystery is the passing over of the transformed self into the loss of self as a fixed point of reference; of *who* God is into *all that* God is. The dismantling of the false self and the inward journey to the true self is the first phase of this transition or passing over. The loss of the true self as a fixed point of reference is the second phase. The first phase results in consciousness of personal union with the Trinity. The second phase consists in being emptied of this union and identifying with the absolute nothingness from

which all things emerge, to which all things return, and which manifests itself as *That-Which-Is*.[125]

We must allow the same. For, death is the dissolution of form. Each time we enter into the nothingness we die, we die to thought forms, to the egoic form, to the form of self, and the final form of being. Allow this phrase to lead you into centering prayer: crucified nothing. Or repeat "crucified nihil, crucified nihil, crucified nihil."

Through contemplation we experience what God in Jesus experienced on the cross. Contemplation is a mystical crucifixion, which means letting the God the Supreme Being vanish. Expanded, it means we consent to God's deconstruction of our world, our ego, our separate-self, and especially God as object to our subject. Let all separation be negated. Allow self to be annihilated into the divine void of godless nothing. There are no gods in the nothing. In fact, there is no "God" as we understand the term. The nothingness transcends God! Beverly Lanzetta comments on this: "Here is the hidden secret of the mystical life, where the soul is admonished to give itself away in imitation of the self-emptying divinity where *God* gives up name and properties."[126] Meister Eckhart describes this as "the quiet desert, into which distinction never gazed, not the Father, nor the Son, nor the Holy Spirit."[127] For him it is the nothingness beyond God. Mystically crucified, both God and us disappear. Through God we surpass God and enjoy mystery beyond mystery without end. Self and God transcended - the realization of ultimate nothingness. And so, savor this shocking phrase: *godless nothing*.

---

[125] Keating, *The Mystery of Christ: The Liturgy as Spiritual Experience*, NY: Continuum, 2001,62.
[126] Lanzetta, 73
[127] *Meister Eckhart: The Essential Sermons*, 198.

*Divine Oneness*

Nothingness can give us a few hints at divine oneness and what it may be like for us. I teased this just before with the phrase *godless nothing*. Here, as always, Jesus and the apophatic mystics are our guides. According to them, oneness with God is not an experience. It is not a thing. It is not like anything we have ever experienced before: "what eye has not seen, ear has not heard, nor what has entered into the human mind."(1 Corinthians 2:9) Let us begin with a personal account. A Carmelite nun named Petra gives her account of divine oneness in Ruth Burrows' book *Guidelines to Mystical Prayer*:

> I seemed to be looking within and I saw that *I* was not there. There was no 'I' I can't say more than that. *I* had gone. It wasn't that I saw or felt God...This was bewildering joy...[her friend Claire responds:] This is really what joy means, isn't it? Nothing but God - and God apparently not there...so that the whole soul is gift, is surrender, is that 'lived nothingness' we spoke of...your experience is of *what you are*.[128]

Being one with God does not mean being one with an object. All the mystics report that God seems to disappear. Meister Eckhart speaks of transcending the Trinity. John of the Cross talks about experiencing abandonment by God. Therese of Lisieux went through a night of nothingness in which God seemed to vanish. The contemporary spiritual author, Bernadette Roberts, helps us make sense of these

---

[128] Burrows, Ruth, *Guidelines to Mystical Prayer*, London: Burns and Oates, 2012, 121-122.

mystical experiences and insights.[129] Roberts holds the position that the journey does not end with mystical union with God. The point of the spiritual journey lies not in the union of the human self with the divine self. Rather, the end is the falling away of self. And this is not the ego self. Once in mystical union, God has already brought the human person beyond ego. Mystical union equals the egoless state. The end as the falling away of self means the dissolution of the true self, of all self. Keating describes the experience of Jesus on the cross in similar terms. Once the self vanishes, God vanishes because God was the object to the self's subject. Even in mystical union we relate to God as "out there," as an object, although this relation is very subtle, because we sense God within. So beyond mystical union we discover the state of no-self. I equate this state with the state of ultimate nothingness.

Roberts' insights on the state of no-self link up with how the apophatic mystics understand oneness with God. Here, let us take Meister Eckhart as the example. Michael Sells discusses Eckhart's understanding of mystical union:

> [It is commonly assumed] that apophatic mystical union is a union 'with God'…in apophatic mystical union reference to the transcendent is undone…that undoing is reflected within language by a disorienting - at certain key points - of standard rules of reference and antecedence. In Eckhart, mystical union occurs when the human soul gives up attachments and images, and when the deity gives up its properties and persons. At this point the deity and the soul revert to the state of

---

[129] see "Introduction" and "Compendium of the Journey," Roberts, Bernadette, *The Experience of No-Self: A Contemplative Journey*, Boulder, CO: Shambala, 1984.

nothingness, out of which and in which the mystical union occurs. Eckhart uses the same word, *eigenschaft*, for both the attachments of the soul and the properties of the deity. *There is no union 'with God'*; rather the union occurs within and beyond the deity. Eckhart writes of the deity as having to give up its own 'properties' in order to be born in the soul in mystical union.[130]

Let us get our terms straight. Sells is discussing mystical union as oneness beyond self. Roberts sees mystical union as the egoless state. They are, in effect, saying close to the same thing: Mystical union is not union at all! Union implies the coming together of two into one. But, the apophatic mystics suggest there is more going on. There is oneness beyond ego and beyond self. When God brings us past ego, we are in union. When God annihilates self, we are one; or, rather, we are *not*, for there is no self left. There is only the nothingness of God. Commenting on Eckhart, Beverly Lanzetta expands on this point:

> [S]alvation is premised on undoing both the ontological structures that make the road possible and the intentioned end of the journey: God. For Eckhart, liberation entails a moment of pure nothingness when God is 'neither this nor that.'...following the soul's movement beyond the Trinity into the secret intimacy of the God beyond God...Admonishing the soul to 'naught' itself, even for one moment, the Meister claims that detachment

---

[130] Sells, Michael, *Mystical Languages of Unsaying*, University of Chicago Press: Chicago, 1994, 12.

leads the soul to experience all the blessedness of its uncreated ground.[131]

Meister Eckhart uses numerous images for the relationship between God and the human person. Three of them are the birth of the Word in the soul, the breakthrough, and the ground. Roughly speaking, we can see the birth of the Word in the soul as the entrance into the egoless state of mystical union and the breakthrough as the passage into the state of no-self. Yet, Eckhart will mix these images up to make sure our conceptions of the journey never become idols. He wants us to rely on nothing but nothing. He wants us to enter into the ground. In Sermon 5b he says, "God's ground is my ground and my ground is God's ground." This means we are always and forever identical with God on the deepest level of reality. In the ground God IS us - even though we are still ourselves. From the understanding of these three images, the spiritual journey becomes a matter of allowing what is most real about us - identity with God - become real in our lives. It is about letting what is within emerge into consciousness then bring us beyond consciousness into the divine identity.

Contemplation transports each of us into the ground, the nowhere of the God within God. This self-same super-divinity brings each one of us down to the ground through the annihilating grace of the breakthrough. "In Eckhart's mystical breakthrough, a deeper negation occurs that draws the soul beyond the nothingness of God to *nothingness*...mystical experience breaks open to the liberation of consciousness, and to the negation not only of all *conceptual* claims, but to the intradivine negation in which *God* unbecomes."[132] It is about each one of us being

---

[131] Lanzetta, 42-43
[132] *Ibid.*, 70

reduced to nothing through the annihilation of all things blocking the ground. God breaks through and negates all things - especially the self - so I may awaken to the indistinct oneness of the ground wherein I discover I am the nothing beyond God. I realize "I, in my ground, am a 'nothing.'"[133] And the nothing surpasses the divine.

Eckhart wants the soul to transcend even God! In fact, that is God's desire as well. Die to God and be released into the nothingness beyond God. Let go of self and let go of God. In other words, let nothing pure and simple. Relinquish attachment to God as object, as 'out there,' as any-*thing* at all, as being at all. Nothingness means detachment, and it is a thorough detachment. In the process of detaching, I realize God is the absolute and incomprehensible nothing beyond God and that I am this self-same nothingness, too! It is nothingness beyond self and God.

Continuing the apophatic tradition, Kerry Walters, a current spiritual author, describes the great act of realizing our oneness with the divine nothing as the act of at-(n)one-ment. Walters believes that at-(n)one-ment is the fulfillment of the incarnation of God *in us*.[134] When we are completely emptied out through identification with Christ Crucified "the soul reawakens to the no-thing it is."[135] The great act of at-(n)one-ment happens when we realize our nothingness *is* divine nothingness: "the nothingness of God-without unifies with the nothingness of God-within" and it is "the wondrous restoration of our true identity."[136] He cites Eckhart as the authority when he says, "In at-(n)one-ment, 'God is identical

---

[133] Turner, 167
[134] Walters, Kerry, Soul Wilderness: A Desert Spirituality, NY: Paulist Press, 2001, 101.
[135] *Ibid.*, 103
[136] *Ibid.*, 104

with the spirit.'"[137] Our true identity is no-identity: beyond self and God in the nothingness.

Thus, nothingness defies expectations of what divine union is, of what enlightenment is, of what it is like to realize oneness with God. Perhaps we love in hidden ways, unknown to us. We influence others without even knowing it - beyond self-reflection and self-awareness. Maybe divine oneness looks differently in different people? Maybe the way divine love is manifest varies from person to person? We can say, however, that for the apophatic mystics oneness "takes place not between two entities or substances but within a ground of "nothingness," the self-emptying nothingness of the contemplative soul or the beyond-being nothingness of the unmanifest Godhead…'*beyond-ousia*' nothingness."[138] Sells goes further and says that "at the point of mystical union, this nothingness or beyond-beingness cannot be distinguished discursively from mere nothingness."[139] Oneness with God is not 'with God' in the sense of 'with another object.' Oneness transcends all duality, all distinction. We really do not know what oneness is, although it lies beyond ego and self, and even divinity.

Apophasis does not mean union with God but in contemplative silence: nothingness. Oneness with God is not the union of two beings - substances - but reverting to the state beyond being within the ground of nothingness: the self-annihilating nothingness of God and the soul as well as the beyond-being nothingness of God, all of which is simply nothing! So, the spiritual journey is about the annihilation of us, what we think is us, into/in/as the nothing. It is the annihilation of our form to allow the already given formlessness to "appear." Again, the end of the journey is

---

[137] *Ibid.*, 105
[138] Sells, 169
[139] *Ibid.*, 130

not about union with God. But in contemplative silence: nothingness. Awakening happens when we realize our nothingness *is* divine nothingness. It comes about when we realize nothingness is nothingness is nothingness: my nothingness is divine nothingness, divine nothingness is my nothingness and the nothingness transcends all - even God. In unknowing, I realize God and I are one and the same nothing, and that all things are one and the same nothing.

St. John of the Cross gives us this Latin translation of a psalm: *Ad nihilum redactus sum et nescivi.*[140] In English this translates to *I have been reduced to nothing, and I did not know it.* This is what is happening in contemplation. I am being reduced to nothing and I don't even know. It don't experience it (mostly). This is true unknowing, utter nothingness, all grace. Surrender into God's nothingness, be silent within, let go, and wait to awaken to your identity as the very same nothingness. It is dying into the self-same nothingness and rising into the paradisiacal oblivion of mystery. Contemplation is just nothing, effortless nothing, silent nothing, non-reflective nothing, selfless nothing, and same nothing. We start to live in and as the heavenly nothing. In contemplative prayer, only nothingness, the nothingness of non-experience, the divine, and beyond the divine. We are not united with a divine substance, but we are reduced to what we always have been: nihil - the divine nihil. Hence savor this last contemplative word: *nothing*.

I hope you have enjoyed this little book. If there has been any blessing, any insight, any wisdom gleaned from it, God be praised. Thank you for staying with me on this journey into the nothingness of centering prayer, the nothingness of contemplation, and the nothingness of God. May you come to know the transcendent joy who is one with us in Christ Jesus.

---

[140] *The Collected Works of St. John of the Cross*, 172

*One desire: to disappear into the invisible
To dissolve into the incomprehensible void of godless nothing
Annihilated I am nothing
Annihilated I am nothing but nothing beyond nothing ∞
I am Infinite Mercy, Unalterable Splendor,
Rejoicing as divine joy transcending all opposites:
sameness and difference, one yet many, human yet divine
Crucified with Christ: the oblivion and silence of the
nothingness beyond God
One and the same as nothing, I delight;
I am one with God and I AM GOD.*

# Appendix I

# Instruction Prayer for Deepening into Mystical Nothingness

Nothing
Just nothing
Effortlessly let God be God: nothing
Let all you are and all you are doing be nothing.
Let thoughts, experience, self-reflection fade into oblivion.
Let thoughts release themselves; everything passes.
Let the attempt to get somewhere in prayer release itself.
Let the form of your method, however subtle, release itself.
Let the subtle thought of having no thoughts release itself.
If needed, let your sacred symbol return to you;
Otherwise, let the returning dissolve and effortless nothing.
Do not make the nothingness happen;
do not force it as an experience.
Just nothing: totally open and nondual receptivity.
No matter what you experience in prayer, effortless nothing.
When you notice you've been thinking about your thoughts
for most of the prayer period, effortless nothing.
Let your mind be blank.
Let your self be the same as the nothing.
Let the nothingness awaken as you.
Divine nothingness is my nothingness;
my nothingness is divine nothingness.
Vanish into Nothing; Sheer Nothing;
Just Nothing; Effortless Nothing; Let Nothing
Silent Nothing; Open Nothing;
Happy Nothing; Merciful Nothing;
Non-thinking Nothing; Non-reflective Nothing; Selfless Nothing;
Singular Nothing; Crucified Nothing; Divine Nothing;
Same Nothing; Godless Nothing;
Nothing

# Appendix II

# Commentary on "Instruction Prayer for Deepening into Mystical Nothingness"

Below is a series of reflections and comments on the "Instruction Prayer for Deepening into Mystical Nothingness." The commentary repeats and summarizes many key themes presented throughout this little book. Savor them, and enjoy.

*Nothing*
*Just nothing*
*Effortlessly let God be God: nothing*
*Let all you are and all you are doing be nothing.*
*Let thoughts, experience, self-reflection fade into oblivion.*

**Nothing**: This opening line sets the tone. The instruction prayer is all about *nothing*. No thoughts, no feelings, no experiences, not even being itself. The rest of the instruction unpacks the mystical nothingness.

**Just nothing**: This instruction is about "just nothing" - no more, no less (literally!). Nothing is added to nothing. It is about giving way to the wisdom of nothingness and letting that wisdom transform your practice of contemplative prayer and your life as well.

**Effortlessly let God be God: nothing**: Here is the call to allow God to be who God is: nothing. Let God be the Mystery of Loving Nothingness. It is an apophatic call to stop projecting onto God our thoughts, feelings, experiences, and even to desist from engaging God as on object to our subject. Stop referring to God as a thing. Stop treating God as a being. Surrender all labels, names, and images of God. God is much more than we think, more than we *can* think.

God transcends all being. Hence, God is nothing. Let God be nothing.

**Let all you are and all you are doing be nothing**: Just allow everything about you, all your focus, your very consciousness, and all you are doing to fade away. Without trying, give yourself over to interior emptiness. Let the activity of the senses and emotions, memories of the past, and worries about the future become nil. Put aside the commotion outside of you and inside of you. Do not think of anything; do not think at all.

**Let thoughts, experience, self-reflection fade into oblivion**: Let the internal dialogue dissolve into nothing. Meet thoughts, feelings, and experiences with nothing. Disregard all thought, all thinking. Have an attitude of non-involvement with the self. Let the self fade away into the void. Yet, who you are is still in the void. We let our thinking dissolve into nothingness and we remain in the nothingness. It is only in mindless oblivion that we realize we are the divine void of godless nothing.

*Let thoughts release themselves; everything passes.*
*Let the attempt to get somewhere in prayer release itself.*
*Let the form of your method, however subtle, release itself.*
*Let the subtle thought of having no thoughts release itself.*

**Let thoughts release themselves; everything passes**: Thoughts are only obstacles to God if we let them be obstacles to God. Thoughts will pass by on their own. They will come, yes. And, they will go – as long as we let them keep going. There are no obstacles to God, not even thoughts.[141] Thoughts do not have to be obstacles to God. Do not give them that kind of power over you. Just let them dissolve. Thoughts are only obstacles in the nothingness if

---

[141] see Frenette, ch.7

you turn them into obstacles. Do not get involved with any content of your mind. Some particular obstacles in contemplative practice might be trying to achieve something during contemplative prayer, becoming attached to a method, or trying to achieve the consciousness of not having any thoughts.

**Let the attempt to get somewhere in prayer release itself**: Ease your effort and stop trying to achieve something when praying. You do not have to do anything at all in prayer. In fact, trying to do something is counterproductive and ego-enhancing. So, allow the attempt, the trying to keep going. It is but a thought. Let it pass through you. The ego-game of achievement and success is not only irrelevant, but also harmful to contemplative practice. We want to prove ourselves worthy. This attitude displaces receptivity. For, it is all about receiving a gift: God. And, it is all God. God does it all. We do nothing.

**Let the form of your method, however subtle, release itself**: Let God nullify any attachment to the form of your method. In other words, let go of the sacred symbol. Even let go of returning to the sacred symbol. Allow everything you initiate to vanish. Let the thought of returning release itself. By letting all thoughts release themselves we have nothing left to do! We can just enjoy the nothingness! We rest in the nothingness. Better still, we do not do anything at all, rather, just nothing.

**Let the subtle thought of having no thoughts release itself**: Being aware of having no thoughts is still a thought. It is self-reflection. We allow the thought of self, the final thought, to pass and release itself. So, disengage from thoughts and self-reflection without seeing them as problems. Let self-reflective thoughts release themselves. Let God free you of the reflective-self. More than a thought, we let God annihilate the unconscious mechanism of self-reflection: the mind's ability to bend back on itself, to know itself as an object. Allow the nothing to destroy this mechanism. Practically speaking, just permit nothingness.

*If needed, let your sacred symbol return to you;*
*Otherwise, rest from returning and effortless nothing.*
*Do not make the nothingness happen;*
*do not force it as an experience.*

**If needed, let your sacred symbol return to you**: Still, in the nothingness we may need our symbol. We may still get hooked on a thought, actively block a thought, or react emotionally to a thought. It is normal! In this case, follow Guideline 3: when engaged with your thoughts, return ever-so-gently to your sacred symbol. To be more receptive, follow Frenette's modification of Guideline 3: "let the sacred word ever so gently return to you."[142] You may also follow his teaching on the sacred breath: when engaged with your thoughts, "return to your breathing."[143] Or, use the sacred gaze: "when engaged with your thoughts, ever so gently turn to God's unseen presence within."[144]

**Otherwise, let the returning dissolve and effortless nothing**: However, you may not need the symbol. In that case, just rest in the naked nothingness. Take a "rest from thinking."[145] Take a break from returning to the symbol. Without effort, without thinking, simply nothing.

**Do not make the nothingness happen; do not force it as an experience**: Remember that the nothingness is not an experience, but rather the negation of experience. The nothingness is below, underneath, beyond, and above our experience because the nothing is divine, and God transcends

---

[142] Frenette, 28
[143] *Ibid.*, 55
[144] *Ibid.*, 62
[145] see Frenette, ch.3

everything. We cannot make the nothingness happen. We cannot create it as an experience. That, again, is to turn nothing into something, into an object. Rather, nothingness is grace! It is God's Gift because the nothing is God as God is in Godself. So, do not, under any circumstance, attempt to create an experience of nothingness or force yourself to think nothing. The emphasis here is on self-initiated activity, which, as was said earlier, only inflates ego and adds more self where there ought to be no self.

*Just nothing: totally open and nondual receptivity.*
*No matter what you experience in prayer, effortless nothing.*
*When you notice you've been thinking about your thoughts for most of the prayer period, effortless nothing.*

**Just nothing: totally open and nondual receptivity**: Nothingness does not split reality into two as does our normal everyday self-consciousness: subject versus object. Nothingness is indistinction, hence utter sameness. At the same time, nothingness is spacious and unreservedly open. That is our stance, which is not a stance (a thing) at all: utter receptivity and nonduality.

**No matter what you experience in prayer, effortless nothing**: You will have many experiences during contemplative prayer: delightful, scary, negative, ecstatic. Ignore them all. Disregard all experience, but with gentleness and compassion. Do not get involved in your experience. Let all experiences pass, whether they are unwanted thoughts and feelings or pleasant thoughts and feelings. Let even religious experiences pass. They are not God. Nothing is better than nothing.

Beware of experientialism in apophatic prayer. This is seeking experiences of the negative because one abhors the experiential vacuum of the apophatic. It means I want to fill the nothingness with psychological experiences - seeking them, seeking objects opposed to the nothingness. We think such negative experiences are achievable, and that they can be induced by practicing some technique. Centering prayer is not a technique, though. It is a method. A method of prayer does not lead us in the direction of experientialism, because it is open-ended and does not seek experiences. Remember the nothingness is not a negative experience but the negativity of experience, the absence of experience. The nothingness negates experience, the experience which treats God as an object of consciousness and a thing to be experienced. The nothingness has nothing to do with this God-object. Only nothingness.

**When you notice you've been thinking about your thoughts for most of the prayer period, effortless nothing**: There will be times when it feels like all you did was think about your thoughts. We can avoid a lot of guilt and self-judgment if we effortlessly allow nothingness when this happens. It will happen. The question is how to handle it when it does. Handle this feeling of failure at meditation with effortless nothing. By "effortless nothing" I mean, without effort allow the nothing. Sink into nothing. No judgment, no getting into our guilt feelings, just nothing.

*Let your mind be blank.*
*Let your self be the same as the nothing.*
*Let the nothingness awaken as you.*
*Divine nothingness is my nothingness;*
*my nothingness is divine nothingness.*

**Let your mind be blank**: Do not try to make your mind a blank, just let it become blank. This, however, is a relative blankness, for there will often still be thoughts passing through your awareness. We are not giving them any attention, though. We are the blankness - the divine underneath thoughts, feelings, experiences, and being.

**Let your self be the same as the nothing**: Who you are is rooted in God. In fact, you are one with God, and God is nothing. Therefore, just as God is the mystery of nothingness - infinite freedom and joy, peace, spaciousness, gratuitousness, and love - so are you, in your deepest reality, the mystery of divine nothingness. So allow that to be true, but not through a mental game. Do not think about it. Accept it in faith. Accept it in unknowing and allow what is true to be true: you are one and the same as the nothing.

**Let the nothingness awaken as you**: The nothing is your deepest self. We are dreaming that we are separate from the nothing. Just wake up! Allow the divine awakening to happen. You will awaken as the divine nothing only in letting yourself be reduced to nothing and in surrendering to the nothing, who is, paradoxically, your real Self.

**Divine nothingness is my nothingness; my nothingness is divine nothingness**: Again, the nothingness deeper than your self is divine. The inner nothingness of contemplative prayer IS the divine reality. But, again, don't focus on any inner experience of nothingness. This inner nothingness transcends or is deeper than experience.

*Vanish into Nothing; Sheer Nothing;*
*Just Nothing; Effortless Nothing; Let Nothing*

**Vanish into Nothing**: Let your very self disappear. Surrender to the nothing without "looking" at anything outside or inside yourself, not holding on to anything, without letting anything hold you, without focusing on anything.

**Sheer Nothing**: Utterly gratuitous nothingness: nothingness for the taking, literally! This requires nothing but openness to nothing. So, sweep away everything inside and outside. Let presence, attention, and intention fall away into the emptiness of the divine void. And remain there.

We can objectify God through our intention. We can treat God as a goal for us to get. Our intention may be used as a means to an end. Whereas, if our intention is just God - read here, just nothing - we can shed this objectifying attitude and let God really be God: mystery beyond mystery beyond all the limitations of our language, of our thinking, of our experience, and even of being. Language can limit our experience of God - making us expect God to be a certain way, to act a certain way, and when it doesn't happen like we expect we may lose faith.

**Just Nothing**: Again, a restatement that it is only nothing - nothing added! Simply and purely nothing! Just nothing means staying in the interior desert, staying in the nakedness of God's love.

**Effortless Nothing**: There is to be no trying, no work, no force, and no effort at all from the self. Allow your very effort to be undone, your very self to be undone. Patiently wait in the nothingness.

**Let Nothing**: Our primary attitude is one of allowing the nothing, permitting the nothing to come, to awaken. Total letting go is the way to open to God. Letting go involves both the intellect and the will. The intellect has to be free of all images and ideas, totally empty with regard to thought. The will has to be free and empty of all desire. Then, God can enter a person's life because there are no objects in the person's life, whether the objects are emotional, material, or psychological. We also let be. This is deeper and more receptive than letting go. It is a matter of non-involvement. We do not even involve ourselves in the process of letting go. We allow God to fee us from attachments. We simply let all our attachments be: all thoughts and experiences and images. Now, deepest of all, we let nothing. We sink from letting go to letting be to letting nothing. We let being itself unravel. In the nothingness letting go and letting be dissolve. Nothingness remains.

Beneath thoughts, feelings, experiences, and even being itself: nothing. Beyond all complications and complexities lies the emptiness of the transcendent. In prayer and life: the simple and gentle void of divine oblivion. We let nothingness in. We allow nothingness to replace our efforts and thoughts and feelings. Allow nothingness to rise up within and reign interiorly. Let go, let be, let nothing. This is the activity of grace rather than anything of our doing. Frenette teaches, "Let God within you let go."[146] More receptive: Let God let God be God. *Let nothing* signifies the vanishing of thought - even if there are still thoughts! While remaining nothing, let thoughts vanish into the nothing.

### *Silent Nothing; Open Nothing; Happy Nothing; Merciful Nothing*

**Silent Nothing**: The nothingness contains no thing at all. There is only utter freedom and joy. Silence is the sole "feature" of nothingness - no noise, no sound, no thoughts, no feelings - only the restful savor of absence, which transcends experience. The silence of sound, thinking, and self enables the transcendence of consciousness and duality.

The silent nothing is the silence of faith. Faith is the apophatic moment in our experience of prayer - it is the negativity of experience. Though the nothing transcends or is deeper than experience, we still have experiences while praying. "This faith de-centers us, for it disintegrates the experiential structures of selfhood on which, in experience, we center ourselves, and at the same time draws us into the divine love where we are re-centered upon a ground beyond

---

[146] *Ibid.*, 166

any possibility of experience. There is, at the center of our selfhood, a ground which is unknowable, even to us. Therefore, that ground on which we are centered is both Love and, as far as our experience goes, Nothing."[147]

**Open Nothing**: In this nothingness we are totally receptive, as has been said. Utter spaciousness is utter freedom to love and not be bound by any obstacle to love. Attachments ease as the firm grasp we had on our possessions slowly opens and allows pure space to replace our inordinate fixation on any particular thing - even God, even nothingness.

**Happy Nothing**: There is a deep, subtle, and very spiritual joy which springs up from this nothingness beyond and beneath being. It is not so much a feeling of happiness as a grounding joy that no words can describe or feelings express. It is divine joy, and, as such, beyond all experience - yet it can, and does, bubble up into experience. Further, we find that we can be happy in nothing, happy with nothing, and supremely happy as nothing.

**Merciful Nothing**: The nothing is fantastic grace and out-of-control mercy, which swallows up our perceived and even unperceived failings, weaknesses, and sin. In being annihilated by the nothing our very sins are used in our favor. Then, all our sin is annihilated.

Further, the good news of divine mercy does not just that God forgives our sins, but that God became one of us so that we might become God. God shows mercy, ultimately, by including us in the divine happiness of the Godhead beyond God. What mercy! God's mercy is revealed in not just giving us a share in the divine joy, but in having us identifying with the mystery and nothingness of divine mercy. Indeed, this very mercy and joy is God's *I am* - the very divine self. Because this merciful delight is God's very

---

[147] Turner, 251

reality, then we cannot define it or understand it for we cannot understand what it is for God to be God.

### *Non-thinking Nothing; Non-reflective Nothing; Selfless Nothing; Singular Nothing*

**Non-thinking Nothing**: By the grace of letting go of all thinking we allow for detachment from all content and all consciousness. While there still may be thoughts travelling through our minds, we are deeper than all thinking and all consciousness. Contemplation is un-thinking nothingness. There is no more active thinking. In transcending thinking, and allowing nothingness we are brought deeper than consciousness itself. Self-reflection may still be functioning, but we are deeper in the nothingness. For, the journey does not end in consciousness (union) but beyond consciousness in the nihil-identity.

**Non-reflective Nothing**: Nothingness is deeper than self-reflection. We gradually drop the self-reflective apparatus of the mind by letting the nothing in, letting the nothing awaken and negate this very structure of the mind. In so doing, nothingness frees us from possessiveness. Noticing when you are engaged with your thoughts is itself a thought - let this vanish into nothing as well. Do not even let your instructions become obstacles or "create" an "experience" of nothingness in centering prayer. Let it all become void and nonexistent. Let it all be not.

**Selfless Nothing**: There is no self in the nothing, for the reflective self and self-consciousness (which is unconscious and dualistic) are negated and transcended. We forget self, not by our own efforts, but through the annihilating grace of God. By grace, we forget that we exist. We do not look at either self or God. Only the blankness of the contemplative void remains. Do not worry about whether "this" is God.

**Singular Nothing**: The nothingness is one, one beyond one. Neither unity nor difference, the one nothing unites all in a paradoxical sameness-yet-distinctness. All creation preserves distinction yet IS the nothing. As we let our oneness with the divine nothing become real, our very consciousness breaks up. Its structures of perception, intellection, and experience are annihilated and transcended in the voiding of experience and the oblivion surpassing being. This nothingness, this negation of negation and negation of experience, transcends all opposites: affirmation and negation, difference and sameness, union and identity. The nothingness negates difference, and so negates the negation between sameness and difference. Allow nondual nothingness.

*Crucified Nothing; Divine Nothing; Same Nothing; Godless Nothing; Nothing*

**Crucified Nothing**: The nothingness of contemplation is identified with Christ's crucifixion and with God. Thus, contemplation participates in the death of Jesus and leads one into God, beyond ego self. Contemplation is about dying into the self-same nothingness. It remains for us to die with Christ Crucified. We must undergo crucifixion to be brought to resurrected life. Being crucified is the radical path of descent that involves letting go at every moment. In imitation of Jesus we let go of all to encounter the Mystery we call "God." In our prayer this means interior silence: allowing all thinking and even the self to fall away simply to sink into God. As we sink deeper and deeper into nothingness, we breakthrough consciousness into nihil-identity: we are the nothing. We die to "God" and penetrate into the God beyond God. Crucified with Christ I vanish into the void of godless nothing.

**Divine Nothing**: God is nothing, transcendent mystery, mystery beyond mystery beyond mystery, divinity beyond God, ever-incomprehensible, utterly infinite and unknowable, transcends existence and being itself. God is not an object, a name, an experience. God does not exist as we understand the term. All of our references to God fall short of the divinity. Let God be mystery; let God be nothing.

**Same Nothing**: Contemplation strips away all differences between us and God. We become indistinguishable from God. Only nothingness is indistinguishable; and God is nothing. The nothingness beyond all is 'where' all are indistinct, all are the same.

**Godless Nothing**: There are to be no gods at all in the nothing: not even images sanctioned by our churches, religions, and theologies. It is no thing you can think of, no supreme being, not being at all. Let self annihilate; let God annihilate - just nothing. We treat God as an object. In fact, all our loves can be objectifying, whether love for God, others, ourselves, or creation. God is not an object outside us to be experienced on our terms. Language for God attempts to grasp God and bring God into our territory, to meet God on our terms. Whereas, apophasis opens to meeting God on God's terms: mystery! When we treat God as an object we make God into something we can experience on our terms.

Further, nothingness transcends God. Surrender your god and sink into the nothing beyond God. Let God vanish from your experience, your life, your very self. Let union with God be reduced to nothing because the journey does not end there. The journey continues into the great and grand nothing beyond all things, beyond all beyonds.

**Nothing**: When you think of self, allow the nothingness. Let yourself become lesser, low, nothing. Absolute Nothingness. The nihility beyond all beyonds obliterates attachments, possessions, ego. We are pulled out of our comfort zones, private time, and fear. There is no exclusion, no boundary, no revenge, no brooding, and no violence. Nor are there comparisons, goals, expectations, assumptions, agendas, or excuses. Delighting in the pure contemplation of the Godhead attention, perception, experience, thought, feeling, judgment, and self-reflection are left behind. No self, no being, only nothing. Let God annihilate your mind, your self, and even God! Relax into nothingness. Repose in the naked nothingness. Remain nothing. Let self and God be annihilated. Beyond union, beyond self, beyond God: just nothing.

But, for one last time, this is not about experiencing nothing - in other words, aiming to experience nothingness as an object. Do not pay attention to any experience. Nothingness is about the negation of experience, for the nothing is deeper than or beyond experience even as the nothing transcends being itself. So, do not at all focus on having an experience of silence, rest, darkness, or even nothingness. We cannot experience nothing. Nothing is transcendent mystery beyond all thought, beyond all feeling, beyond all experience, beyond all dualism, and beyond all being. *Experience* keeps us locked in dualism: the subject experiences an object. *Being* also keeps us within the confines of dualism: I am a being, others are beings opposed to me, even prayer as being present to God implies two discrete subjects and not the oblivion of nondual nothingness. Nothing is deeper than being. Often contemplative practice is described as "just being." Just nothing transcends just being: just being still implies self is maintained, whereas just nothing involves the dissolution of the boundaries around the self so that one disappears into the void beyond divinity.

I am not peddling an experience of nothing, as if we could experience nothing as an object—like we might experience anything in the world. God, the nothing, transcends experience. Rather, the nothing serves to negate experience and even the sameness and difference that prevail between beings (creatures) and between beings and God. The nothing negates experiences of nothingness as well as a theology of nothingness and dualistic consciousness itself. The nihil negates God: any talk of or names for God. Transcending a separate God, the nothing opens out into the vast space of infinite mercy. This is the nothing beyond God. In this we are transformed. We receive freedom from self - all by God's free gift. Non-thinking godless nothing is simple nonduality beyond awareness. Ultimately, it is all nothingness: gratuitously good and divine love. This is unlimited happiness, our definitive blessing. God: nothing but nothing beyond nothing $\infty$.

# Bibliography

Angelus Silesius, *The Cherubinic Wanderer*, NY: Paulist Press, 1986.

Anonymous, *The Cloud of Unknowing*, ed. James M. Walsh, SJ, NY: Paulist Press, 1981.

Anonymous, The Cloud of Unknowing, Brewster, Mass.: Paraclete Press, 2006. Kindle Edition.

Burrows, Ruth, *Guidelines to Mystical Prayer*, London: Burns and Oates, 2012.

Chomsky, Noam, *Profit Over People: Neoliberalism and Global Order*, NY: Seven Stories Press, 1999. Kindle Edition.

Duclow, Donald, "Divine Nothingness and Self-Creation in John Scotus Eriugena," *The Journal of Religion*, Volume 57, Number 2, April 1977.

Francis of Assisi, *Francis of Assisi: The Saint*, NY: New City Press, 1999.

Frenette, David, *The Path of Centering Prayer*, Boulder, CO: Sounds True, 2012.

Groody, Daniel G., *Globalization, Spirituality, and Justice*, NY: Orbis Books, 2007. Kindle Edition.

Harmless, William, *Desert Christians: An Introduction to the Literature of Early Monasticism*, NY: Oxford University Press, 2004. Kindle Edition.

Henry Suso, *Henry Suso: The Exemplar with Two German Sermons*, trans. And ed. Frank Tobin, NY: Paulist Press, 1989.

Keating, Keating, *Invitation to Love: The Way of Christian Contemplation*, NY: Continuum, 1998.

— *The Mystery of Christ: The Liturgy as Spiritual Experience*, NY: Continuum, 2001.

— *Manifesting God*, NY: Lantern Books, 2005.

— *Open Mind, Open Heart: The Contemplative Dimension of the Gospel*, NY: Continuum, 2006.

— *Intimacy with God*, NY: Crossroad, 2009.

— *Meditations on the Parables of Jesus*, NY: Crossroad, 2010.

— "Centering Prayer and Resting in God," Contemplative Outreach News, Vol.29 #1, December 2012.

Lanzetta, Beverly, *The Other Side of Nothingness: Toward a Theology of Radical Openness*, Albany, NY: State University of New York Press, 2001.

*Letters of St. Therese of Lisieux Volume II*, trans. John Clark, Washington, DC: ICS Publications, 1988.

*Meister Eckhart: The Essential Sermons, Commentaries, Treatises, and Defense*, trans. Edmund Colledge, NY: Paulist Press, 1981.

*Meister Eckhart: Teacher and Preacher*, ed. Bernard McGinn, NY: Paulist Press, 1986.

Moore, Thomas, *Meditations: On the Monk Who Dwells in Daily Life*, NY: Harper Collins, 1994.

Nemeck, Frances Kelly, and Coombs, Marie Theresa, *Contemplation*, Eugene, OR: Wipf and Stock, 1982.

Perl, Eric David, *Theophany: The Neoplatonic Philosophy of Dionysius the Areopagite*, Albany, NY: State University of New York Press, 2007. Kindle Edition.

*Pseudo-Dionysius: The Complete Works*, trans. Colm Luibheid, NY: Paulist Press, 1987

Roberts, Bernadette, *The Experience of No-Self: A Contemplative Journey*, Boulder, CO: Shambala, 1984.

Rohr, Richard, *The Naked Now*, NY: Crossroad, 2009.

Sells, Michael, *Mystical Languages of Unsaying*, Chicago: University of Chicago Press, 1994.

*The Collected Works of St. John of the Cross*, trans. Kieran Kavanaugh and Otilio Rodriguez, Washington, DC: ICS Publications, 1991.

*The Complete Mystical Works of Meister Eckhart*, trans. Maurice O'C. Walshe, revised by Bernard McGinn, Crossroad: NY, 2009.

*The Divine Names and The Mystical Theology*, trans. John D. Jones, Marquette University Press: Milwaukee, WI, 1999.

*The Gospel of Thomas: The Hidden Sayings of Jesus*, trans. Marvin Meyer, Saying 97, Harper Collins: NY, 1992.

*The Wisdom of Meister Eckhart*, ed. Jan Srtyz, New Grail Publishing: St. Paul, MN, 2003.

Tolle, Eckhart, *The Power of Now*, Vancouver, B.C. and Novato, CA: Namaste and New World Publishing, 1999.

Turner, Denys, *The Darkness of God: Negativity in Christian Mysticism*, Cambridge University Press: Cambridge, 1995.

Walters, Kerry, *Soul Wilderness: A Desert Spirituality*, Paulist Press: NY, 2001

Printed in Great Britain
by Amazon

Published May 2014